Rain, Steam, and Speed

# Rain, Steam, and Speed

**BUILDING FLUENCY IN**

**ADOLESCENT WRITERS**

Gerald Fleming
Meredith Pike-Baky

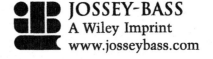

JOSSEY-BASS
A Wiley Imprint
www.josseybass.com

Published by Jossey-Bass
A Wiley Imprint
989 Market Street, San Francisco, CA 94103-1741    www.josseybass.com

Jossey-Bass books and products are available through most bookstores. To contact Jossey-Bass directly, call our Customer Care Department within the U.S. at 800-956-7739, outside the U.S. at 317-572-3986, or fax 317-572-4002.

Jossey-Bass also publishes its books in a variety of electronic formats. Some content that appears in print may not be available in electronic books.

**Library of Congress Cataloging-in-Publication Data**

Fleming, Gerald J., 1946-
  Rain, steam, and speed : building fluency in adolescent writers / Gerald Fleming, Meredith Pike-Baky.
    p. cm. — (The Jossey-Bass education series)
  Includes bibliographical references and index.
  ISBN 0-7879-7456-0 (alk. paper)
  1. English language—Composition and exercises—Study and teaching (Middle school) 2. English language—Composition and exercises—Study and teaching (Secondary)  I. Pike-Baky, Meredith, 1948–
II. Title. III. Series.
  LB1631.F616 2004
  808'.042'0712—dc22

                             2004014540

FIRST EDITION

          10 9 8 7 6 5 4 3 2

The Jossey-Bass Education Series

# CONTENTS

R*ain, Steam, and Speed* is a comprehensive framework of instructional protocols intended to expand and deepen students' written fluency. It is a year-long curriculum that builds students' self-confidence, self-awareness, and knowledge of the world. It increases the students' abilities to write easily and articulately on personal and abstract topics. This journal-writing program takes just over an hour per week of instructional time and can easily be integrated into a broader writing framework.

The first of the three integral components of the program is *Rain,* which involves establishing the climate and includes an essential music strand that enables deep focus and steady writing. The second component, *Steam,* is composed of the *prompts,* the 150 writing departure points that tap students' interests and open them to the larger world. The final component, *Speed,* is the carefully structured routine for writing that students follow twice a week.

The book includes a detailed discography of recommended and easily accessed CDs. The prompts are organized thematically and feature issues that range from imaginative to serious, reflecting the preoccupations of young people today. Support for teachers in implementing the program is abundant and includes grading and assessment guidance. Word-for-word teacher instructions as well as explanations of rationale for each component of the program make this book both easy to follow and entertaining to read.

The prompts in *Rain, Steam, and Speed* are carefully designed and structured to provide a variety of "access points," so that high-school and middle-school students of varied abilities and experience in writing can respond immediately. The prompts offer content vocabulary and guiding questions to enable a substantial response. From the structure of the prompts, student entries become increasingly developed expository pieces. In this way, the journal writing begun in *Rain, Steam, and Speed* can become the foundation of an expository writing program.

*Rain, Steam, and Speed* sets out to change the way teachers think about the dynamics of journal writing. It reflects the refinements of nearly twenty years of classroom practice. Student examples and commentaries woven throughout *Rain, Steam, and Speed* show how student writers in grades 6 through 12 can find engaging topics that are "fun to write about" and make it easy to write "more every time," as students themselves report.

## ACKNOWLEDGMENTS

The authors would like to thank the following people for their kind help on this project—whether recently or historically: Elliott Barenbaum, Candice Fukumoto, David Pan, Mary K. Sayle, Geoff Bernstein, Richard Shaw, Elf Diggerman, Maria Canoy, Marshall Johnson, Geraldine Fleming, Gabe Fleming, Bernie Fleming, Jessica Fleming, Eric Sorensen, Dartanyan Brown, Cathryn Bruno, Susan Price, Pam Berkman, Sarah Baky, Beth Morton, Alice Gosak Gary, Helen Kalkstein Fragiadakis, Tascha Folsoi, Alex Baky, Audrey Fielding, Marty Williams, Marean Jordan, and Carol Tateishi.

Our thanks to Jossey-Bass editor Christie Hakim for her enthusiastic support of *Rain, Steam, and Speed.*

Finally, deep thanks to the students who participated directly in this book, and to those many student writers over the years—brave apprentices!—whose energy propels *Rain, Steam, and Speed.*

## ABOUT THE AUTHORS

**Gerald Fleming** teaches English, social studies, and journalism at Marina Middle School in San Francisco. He has taught in the San Francisco Public Schools for more than thirty years, and he attributes part of the success of the program described in *Rain, Steam, and Speed* to his decade in early childhood education, where talking with kids, recognizing their interests, and building from their own realities are essential skills.

He has published poetry widely (a collection is forthcoming next spring from Sixteen Rivers Press), for five years edited and published the literary magazine *Barnabe Mountain Review,* and has published other books for teachers, *Keys to Creative Writing* (Allyn & Bacon, 1991) among them. He served as a mentor teacher for many years, received the Golden Apple Fellowship from the San Francisco Education Fund/U.C. Berkeley in 2000, and that same year was named Bay Area Middle School Teacher of the Year by San Francisco State University. In addition to his full-time position at Marina, he teaches part-time at the University of San Francisco. He has done teacher training throughout California, has just completed a general-audience book on the life of a public school teacher, and is at work on *How to Teach Middle School and Live to Tell the Tale.*

**Meredith Pike-Baky** coordinates professional development, designs writing performance assessments, and works as a classroom coach for Education Task Force in Larkspur, California. She began teaching more than thirty years ago as a Peace Corps Volunteer in Togo, West Africa, and attributes her passion for student-centered learning to this early experience. She believes in the importance of guiding students to become thinkers through writing and considers *Rain, Steam, and Speed* a seminal contribution to this effort.

She has written for several publishers: *Task Reading* for Cambridge University Press (1981); *Worldbeat, Mosaic Writing I,* and *Mosaic Writing II* for McGraw-Hill; and *Tapestry Writing I* and *Tapestry Writing II* for Heinle & Heinle. She has traveled widely as a workshop leader and visiting author and is currently developing writing courses for teachers.

Rain, Steam, and Speed

# Entering a Zone of Civility

It was near the end of the school year, late May, and I had visited Jerry Fleming's classes many times before. I remembered the first time, fifteen years earlier, in fact, reading a children's picture book from a stool at the front of the classroom and using visual and textual content to plant the seeds of cross-cultural awareness. Throughout the years Jerry and I had schemed and cotaught many lessons on reading more deeply, writing more elaborately, and developing student-friendly scoring guides. The visits that were most compelling, however, were those when I stepped into "Journal Time" and observed the most remarkable sustained student writing I had ever seen. The writing was not only striking in its process but in the results it yielded, its product, so I invited Jerry to present the program to teachers from the large K–12 multi-district consortium in which I work. I listened as Jerry described the evolution of *Rain, Steam, and Speed.* I looked again at the compelling pre and post student writing samples and tried out some of the prompts on my own. Finally, I watched as other teachers implemented this unique fluency development program and got dramatic results. I was convinced that Jerry *had to* share the success of his program with others. So here I was again, to chronicle, in detail, what took place in the classroom.

Today I tried to "look again for the first time." I watched students of many diverse backgrounds enter and take their seats. They sat in two sets of two rows facing each other and took out pens as a student monitor distributed their journal folders. Classroom décor reflected the tastes and travels of an educator who views his classroom as a window to the world for students. There was something interesting to see everywhere I looked on the unusually high walls (the school is a WPA building, nearly seventy years old). I saw a huge photographic mural of an alpine lake, lots of art posters (Picasso's *Guernica,* another celebrating the Spanish poet Frederico García Lorca, a Chinese painting of cascading leaves, a Kandinsky print), a Japanese fan, a vase of fresh flowers, student art and writing, and nearly a dozen Asian and African masks. School notices, schedules, cafeteria menus, and reminders to students were posted at student eye-level at the front of the room, and near the entries two signs announced: "You are entering a ZONE OF CIVILITY" and "Si no tiene nada que hacer, no lo venga a hacer aqui." Sets of novels, stacks of textbooks, newspapers, and dictionaries were set in bookcases around the room's perimeter. The classroom gave an impression of inspiration and industriousness.

Students opened their journal folders and prepared to write. The blackboard at the front of the room was filled completely with Jerry's handwriting. Jerry introduced me to the class, asked a student to read the prompt, checked for questions, and immediately students began writing. He wrote: "Kronos Quartet—*Pieces of Africa*" on the tiny whiteboard at the front of the room and started the CD player. Percussive music tooted, tapped, blared, and boomed through melodic phrases as students wrote without interruption for twenty minutes. From time to time a student would pause, read over the page, stretch, sigh, then write more. Most students were still in the middle of a thought when Jerry called "Time" and asked students to complete their last sentence.

I knew, of course, that what I was witnessing was not typical of many middle- or high-school classrooms. Generally, students take anywhere from five to ten minutes to get settled, pull out necessary supplies, complete their conversations from the hallway, lunch break, or previous class, and get down to work. I also knew that it was highly unusual for students to maintain sustained writing for twenty minutes. Many teachers have students keep journals—fifteen minutes was the longest writing period I had witnessed, and more often getting students to write for ten minutes was a "stretch." I was even more convinced that what Jerry had worked to refine and what these students were able to do was worth sharing.

We come to you then, gentle educator, with a remarkable program to develop your students' fluency in writing. And we come to you in three voices: the voice of the practitioner, Jerry, who has developed, revised, and refined the program with a commitment to building on the potential he recognized from its earliest stages. The second voice is mine. I am Meredith, and I interject comments, references, and observations from the perspective of the outside observer, the teacher-coach, and *teacher of writing as teacher of thinking.* In an administrative position for several years, I've had time to work in many  classrooms, keep up on research, and do some studies of my own. (I can take credit for persuading Jerry to share this program.) The third voice, without which the first two would be of questionable credibility, comprises the opinions, perspectives, experiences, and testimonials of the many students who have "journeyed" on *Rain, Steam, and Speed.* You will see that most of these students began with little confidence about themselves as writers and with minimal practice in the sustained exploration and development of ideas on paper. We have woven these three voices throughout the book into a tapestry of enthusiasm for what we have to share. We invite you to read and try *Rain, Steam, and Speed* with your students. Jerry begins by telling you how the program began.

# Moving Journals Beyond the Banal

Twenty years ago I was sent to a tough inner-city school in San Francisco. It served kids from three of the most difficult housing projects in the city, one of which, a high-rise, has since been torn down because of its dangerous conditions.

I was new to teaching English; my preceding decade had been spent in the lovely labor of working with very young children in early childhood education. These new kids—middle-schoolers, some taller than I, many heavier than I—astonished me. They swaggered. They swore. They were quick to anger, both at other students and at teachers. They were tough-skinned (they needed to be), but slowly, over the course of months, revealed an inner tenderness and vulnerability that moved me deeply. They were *kids,* after all, and subject to the same emotional storms kids weather. Only their storms had more torment to them, and often had to do with matters of life and death.

## AN ADMISSION: EARLY ERRORS

A writer, I wanted my students to write—to jump-start a process that could sharpen their articulation. Writing was easy for me, and I wanted them to discover it to be easy. But with a few exceptions, their skills were low. They'd write a sentence where a paragraph was called for, a paragraph instead of a well-developed essay.

Did they have anything to write about? They sure did: day-to-day experiences so deep that I was in awe, experiences that—embarrassed as I am to admit it now—the writer in me envied. Such material!

I'd read a little about kids' having success in writing journals. So why not try journals? A good idea, certain to succeed.

The kids were given folders. *Write "My Journal" on these*, I told them, *and your name*. We were off on our writing adventure, I thought. *Now, for the next five minutes of the period, write in your journal. You can write anything you want.*

What a liberal feeling: empowering students to write their thoughts and feelings. Surely this largesse would engender more fluent writing; surely this would lead to the Elysian fields of write-at-a-moment's-notice fluency. And imagine! A ready-made activity to get kids to settle down during the first five minutes of class!

But instead of focused—or even discursive—mini-essays on the deep love and violence and complexity each student was experiencing every day, here's what I got on Monday:

*I woke up at 7:00 today. Right on time. I ate breakfast. The bus was on time. I was on time for school, but I went to the donut shop so I was late. My teacher yelled.*

Then, on Tuesday,

*I woke up at 7:10 today. My alarm didn't go off. I didn't have time to eat breakfast. But the bus was on time. I was on time for school. No donut shop today. My teacher didn't yell.*

And so on, from student after student, day after day.

Were they writing? Yes, they were writing. And yes, too, the class was quiet for five minutes, the students compliant. But I was disappointed: why wasn't I getting the depth that I sought? Why were their entries so short? Aha: that was it. Too little time!

The next day I announced, *OK, you guys. These journals are really short. I'm going to raise the time to* ten *minutes so that you can get more writing done. So starting today. . . .*

You've probably predicted what I got:

Monday:

*I woke up at 7:00 today. I was really, really, really sleepy. I took a shower. I ate breakfast. It was frosted flakes. The bus was late, so I was late for school. Half an hour late. My teacher got mad. It was my fourth time to be late for her class. She got really mad this time.*

Was it more writing? Sure. Meaningful? Not what I was hoping for: a mere sequential recall of the morning's events. The journals weren't working.

Teachers reading this book have probably had a good laugh already. These were a rookie's mistakes: too little setup ("anticipatory set," as it's sometimes called), instructions far too vague, time far too short, and an overall sense of nonchalance on the teacher's part that invited reciprocal nonchalance in students. Overarching goals? Absent. Assessment? None. Student responsibility? None. *Doomed:* the journals were a dismal failure.

The year proceeded, English-teacher-overwhelm occurred by November, and by January I'd abandoned the journals. *Journals just don't work for me,* I decided, and focused instead on essay practice.

Yet, not surprisingly, my essay practice failed, too. Though I was proudly liberal-minded in allowing students to make copious spelling errors in early drafts and twist their syntax like grammatical contortionists, their essays remained thin in both volume and content: emaciated reflections of who they were as human beings.

A new year started. I took workshops. One workshop turned me on to response journals, sometimes called "dialectical journals," in which kids write, on the left side of a vertically folded paper, a textual quote, and record their responses on the right. There was success with that, and, perhaps desperate for any elicited writing, I used dialectical journals madly, daily, and "ran them into the ground" with the kids. They couldn't stand them after four months.

More workshops, then: about "exchange-response journals," wherein students write, exchange papers with another, write responses, and repeat the process.

Those worked well, but I had a difficult time using exchange journals consistently while controlling what I perceived to be gossip entries. I wanted to give kids freedom, a sense of ownership over their own writing, yet I didn't want my English class to degenerate into a roomful of kids writing teacher-approved notes in class, all under the aegis of "freewriting," rationalized by the idea that kids will achieve fluency and ultimate writing depth if they scribble notes to each other on subjects of their own choosing—often, alas, about crushes on boys, on girls, or about parties. So the peer journals went their way, too, and another year passed.

Another year, another workshop. This time, the presenter, a teacher, casually mentioned that he'd had some recent success in journal entries in which kids needed to write a certain amount in a certain time. The idea intrigued me, but seemed anti-intellectual. It implied that quantity and not quality was important. It seemed to ignore kids who were thoughtful, introspective, or slow thinkers and writers. It was artificial. (And what about subject matter? Could a student be expected to do a genuine "freewrite" given a time and length limit? Wouldn't such an idea kill any modicum of creativity? And how would you grade the darned things?)

Surprisingly, though, when I tried timed freewrites I noticed that about half of my students responded: they rose to the occasion and wrote more volubly than ever before. Some, I was shocked to discover, even ventured past the invisible fence of mere recapitulation of daily routines and out into realm of ideas. *Oh boy, oh boy,* I thought; their journals reflected less a diary gestalt and more an overall sense of "journalness"—a focused, sometimes discursive, lively reflection on a subject I'd suggest.

I was onto something; I knew it. I read: Donald Graves, Lucy Calkins, others. Though the years were passing, I now felt closer to the locus of what I believed was truly elicited, "student-owned" writing.

I made some decisions. I stayed with the timed journal (a good thing), institutionalized it as a twice-weekly activity (another good thing), and succeeded in communicating to kids that the endeavor was important.

But I continued making mistakes, too. The prompts I wrote on the board were sometimes ambiguous and always too short, giving kids little to work with. I expected lots of writing per session, yet was vague on exactly how much was satisfactory. I gave kids too little time to work, and a sense of frustration and hostility gradually arose around the journals. When I increased the time allotted, I began having class management problems in keeping kids quiet. I tried playing music on my cheap stereo boom box, and though it seemed to help, the music sent through those tinny speakers was banal tripe from a limited repertoire.

However, beyond a doubt, I was getting better writing in these journals than ever before—in essay work kids were writing more fluently than previous classes. Nonetheless, the process needed refining. It lacked clarity, and the kids—quite cooperative, really—let me know explicitly and implicitly.

The summer's break gave me time to think. I felt that the skeletal structure of the journal program was strong, but it needed some muscle on its bones. When I went back that next September, things broke loose in these journals, and they've been a wild, wonderful ride ever since—the highest, most joyous experience of my teaching every year.

## WHAT CHANGED?

A few things changed, and their alteration made all the difference. The prompts I wrote on the board were longer, more energetic, their subject matter unafraid; they were multilayered in what they asked of kids. While sticking with the twice-weekly schedule, I increased the time to twenty minutes to give kids room to do what I asked: write long, thoughtful, focused entries.

---

*Usually there are a bunch of questions up on the board. I usually answer each question in a paragraph so everything would be in place. I think the questions really help because it gets us really thinking.*

---

—Anderson Ren

I gave the kids *prerogative:* choose the topic on the board or write on a topic of their own, as long as theirs was on a subject and not a mere laundry list of what they did yesterday or last Tuesday.

---

*I usually write on something else; I don't like to write on the topic. I write fast because I write on things I like, and when it is interesting I can write very fast.*

---

—Betty Yee

It might be second nature to many teachers, but local teacher research has demonstrated the motivational value of giving students choice in learning. Student buy-in to content as well as process grows dramatically when they have an opportunity to make selections about what they will study. (See "Tim's Advice" in Appendix D to read about the power of choice.)

I established clear guidelines for grading, and while retaining my relaxed stance on spelling and syntax (journals are first-draft work, after all), insisted on a modicum of neatness. Finally, I bought a decent but inexpensive stereo and began collecting and playing instrumental music of many genres—each among the best of its kind.

*One thing that really helps is the music. It's not too loud because it doesn't distract me from doing my journal. Actually, it helps me even write more. It makes me feel calm. None of the music has words. If it did, I think it would be distracting.*

—Anderson Ren

I've stayed with it, refined it, queried the kids at midyear and year-end toward improving the process, implemented many of their suggestions, and established in my classroom a program that still stuns me. (As I write this, the picture of my student Teakeysha is still fresh: Teakeysha, who yesterday got my attention during Journal Time, silently holding up her paper, on which in a dozen minutes she'd easily filled an entire side. I see the proud look on her face: Teakeysha—the one who complained mightily when I explained our journal protocol three weeks ago. . . .)

What comes next, then, dear colleague, is a step-by-step rendering of that program, carved with the blade of kids' imperatives: imperatives both voiced by them and communicated behaviorally. This program works if one of your aims is to achieve fluency in student writing, depth in the subject matter, and "drop of a dime" ability in students to write in a way that is either focused or discursive, depending upon the moment's demand.

This journal process has grown as I have grown. In it I have found not only convincing evidence of writing growth in individual students but also a real plumbing of the depths in their writing. And, not least, I've found the bonus of a contagious and communal joy.

So what I'll lay out here is the protocol for what I've come to call Fluency Journals: words on assessing the journals, what works and why it works (sometimes what *doesn't* and why it doesn't), other issues germane to the practice, and enough "prompts" from which to choose for more than an entire school year.

## FLUENCY JOURNALS AS *PRACTICE*

I use the word *practice* less in the sense of repetition—connoting, at its most negative, a child forced to practice piano—and more in the Buddhist sense: a kind of meditation to which one (the teacher, the student) is committed, and to which one attends, is present for, regularly. It is a quiet study: a study for the teacher in getting to know the students deeply, and a study for students in self-discovery.

*I like Journal Time because it's peaceful.*

—Amy Yan

*When Mr. Fleming puts his music on, it's like relaxing your mind and it puts you to think more.*

—Eva Velasquez

Before long, community is created: community not of master and acolytes but of guide and guided: a guide whose role it is to establish and maintain safety, to suggest—even if such suggestions sometimes go ignored by the guided, who, quickly familiar with the lay of the land, feel confident to move on.

*That's* what we're all about, isn't it?

## INSPIRATION FOR THE NAME

The name of the program, *Rain, Steam, and Speed,* is based on a mid-nineteenth-century English painting by J.M.W. Turner. The scene is of a steam train rushing forward through driving rain, framed on one side by people boating, and on the other, by folks plowing a field. The picture is associated with the railway frenzy that swept across England at this time. To us it suggests the power of determination and focus in developing thoughtful literacy.

In the classroom, the "Rain" tying the scene together is the music strand that supports the students' deep focus and steady writing; the "Steam"—the driving force—is the set of prompts that provide writing departure points to tap students' interests and open them to the larger world, and the "Speed" is the momentum built by the structured routine for writing that students follow twice a week. When the rhythm of these three components gets established, we think you will find that your students' writing will become more thoughtful, more correct, and more substantial. In addition, students will develop more confidence as writers and thinkers.

*I would say journal writing has greatly improved my writing because I feel less shy about expressing my ideas and thoughts. . . . Before, I hated expressing my ideas in fear that people would make a public mockery of me or my ideas.*

—Elena Escalante

Through validation, feedback, systematic practice, and examples, students will be able to transfer what they've learned to expository writing assignments and projects in other subjects. Finally, the fluency development program presented here provides significant student support for the demands of the many writing tests required of students.

*This time produces a mind quick to react to any topic given spontaneously, and that would be more than useful in the torturous SAT-9 (standardized test).*

—Charles Kwan

As you observe improved fluency in your students, we hope that *Rain, Steam, and Speed* will alter the way you (teachers!) think about journal writing. Unlike so many journal programs that are largely busywork, lack focus, and present enormous reading demands for teachers without a clearly defined purpose, *Rain, Steam, and Speed* contains a system of accountability that directs improvement and simplifies evaluation. Come explore the simple power of *Rain, Steam, and Speed.*

*I am able to write almost two times as much as I started with. I used to hate writing, but it is different now.*

—George Zhu

# Fluency

## The Missing Ingredient in Writing Instruction

Curiously, fluency in writing is rarely *taught*. Many teachers have students practice activities that help them generate ideas about a certain topic (freewriting, brainstorming, webbing, looping, and other strategies), but such activities are usually quite open-ended, with little guidance for increasing fluency. In addition, the plenitude of journal programs—daily, weekly, bimonthly—all have merit, but most of them are designed to strengthen student-teacher connections, provide an outlet for topics not assigned or formally graded in class, and give the teacher some background (and often critical) information about students' lives outside school. These journals extend an invitation to write freely; they do not necessarily teach fluency.

### WHAT IS WRITING FLUENCY?

Two students sit down to write an in-class essay. The assignment is clear. Both students are interested in the topic and motivated to write well. But as soon as the writing period begins, the students react in quite different ways. One begins writing immediately, head bent over pen and paper. After writing steadily for ten minutes, the student pauses, switches the pen to the other hand and back, stretches, hunches over again, and continues writing. The other student has a much tougher time getting started. This one begins by doodling in the margin of the blank paper, then wipes the pen clean with a paper towel from a jacket pocket and looks distractedly around the room. This student doesn't actually commit pen to paper until ten minutes into the writing period, at last struggling to construct a coherent first paragraph. The difference in these students is obvious: one is a fluent writer; the other is not.

Fluency refers to the ease with which one communicates in each of the language skills. For a student giving an oral presentation, fluency is the ability to talk at a steady pace, choose the right words, approximate correct grammar, and be understood despite any accent or other variation in speech. For a reader, fluency is the ability to read steadily and get the gist of the material. A fluent listener understands with minimal effort what is being said. A fluent writer is able to jot down and develop ideas readily and steadily on paper. Marie Ponsot and Rosemary Deen refer to this as "prolific writing" in *Beat Not the Poor Desk*. "Practiced, prolific writing keeps language and perceptions flowing past the fidgets, self-distractions, and bogeys that the mind occasionally throws out when it doesn't care to work."

Yes, fluency has to do with speed and effort; it is the *facility* with which one uses language in all its forms. Fluent speech can be accented, fluent listening can include gaps in understanding, fluent reading can involve understanding the big idea of a selection without understanding some specific words or expressions. Similarly, fluent writing can have mistakes, but its overall meaning is unmistakable. A fluent writer successfully expresses ideas with steady ease.

## WHY TEACH FLUENCY?

Few students today arrive in our classrooms as fluent writers. Many do not speak English as a first language. Even if they were born in the United States, they often speak a language other than English at home. But it's not only nonnative speakers who have difficulty communicating on paper; native speakers struggle with spontaneous writing, too.

Few teachers realize the importance of teaching fluency, and fewer know how to do it. Current "accountability pressures" reduce the amount of time for teachers to implement comprehensive writing programs that would include fluency development. These same pressures emphasize correctness, often intimidating students who need to try out ideas and take risks with language. Many teachers are asked to implement prescribed writing instruction, skipping the developmentally critical stage of helping students get comfortable as ideas move from head to paper. Generating, developing, and focusing ideas comes with fluency and is the fundamental first stage in the writing process. Indeed, Ponsot and Deen describe "prolific writing" as a "central" and "elemental" skill; it must be systematically taught. Developing fluency is critical to becoming a writer.

In *Teaching Basic Writing: An Alternative to Basic Skills,* David Bartholomae argues that student writers need to imagine themselves as writers. He claims that the failure of writing programs is due, in large part, to a syllabus that is "imposed upon a learner . . . serving the convenience of teachers or administrators" without permitting basic writers "to imagine themselves as writers writing." Critical to effective instruction in writing, according to Bartholomae, is instruction that "allows students to experience the possibilities for contextualizing a given writing situation in their own terms, terms that would allow them to initiate and participate in the process by which they and their subject are transformed" (p. 33).

Students who move through the protocols of *Rain, Steam, and Speed* recognize that they have had authentic writing experiences and opportunities, as Bartholomae describes them, to test and render ideas through their own thinking and experience. Refer to Appendix D and eighth-grader Pamela's final entry of the year to see how she characterized improvement in her thinking and writing.

---

*I believe that journals are useful to a writer because a writer should practice. I bet a lot of writers have journals to get warmed up to write.*

---

—George Zhu

What we risk, I'm afraid, in not teaching fluency, is the production of increasing numbers of high school and college graduates who cannot respond to a writing assignment of any nature with thoughtful agility. We risk turning out students who have little confidence in themselves as literate citizens, able to process questions, problems, issues, or concerns through writing. We risk teaching kids to hate writing. It's not acceptable to leave students doodling in the margins, unable to write. We must teach fluency!

## SUPPORTING ENGLISH LANGUAGE LEARNERS

With the growing number of nonnative speakers in our classrooms, we find that we must design instruction to support students who are learning content and English simultaneously. Many of these students, those in ESL classes as well as those who have been mainstreamed, are fluent speakers but have always shied away from writing. These students have much to gain from *Rain, Steam, and Speed.* It is pointed out in *Journal Writing* (Burton and Carroll, 2001) that "journal writing assists the development of language" (p. 4). The editors cite findings from a study on journals by Fulwiler that emphasize the value of writing. These points are familiar to most of us:

- When students make connections between what they already know and new information, they learn and understand better. (This is called "schema-building.")
- When students write about what they learn, they learn and understand better.
- When students care about what they write, they learn and understand even better.

Burton and Carroll interpret these observations to indicate that "only when people write do they discover what they know," because writing is an instrument of thought as well as a way of recording information. Their observations echo what we have found with nonnative speakers' writing in *Rain, Steam, and Speed.* With compelling topics, a sense of urgency determined by a limited time period in which to write, and the focusing power of the music, second-language learners are able to discover an ease and comfort with English that they find surprising. (Refer to Ya Ni's and Jerry Xie's entries in Appendix D.) Indeed, according to Burton and Carroll, written fluency development results from regular, structured journal writing that incorporates explicit expectations for length and content. *Rain, Steam, and Speed* is particularly effective for second-language learners because it encourages them to take risks with thinking and language. It helps them develop "a personal voice, a sense of audience, and the confidence to explore identity."

## CORRECTNESS: WHERE DOES IT FIT IN A FLUENCY PROGRAM?

We know that, with its need for speed, ease, and maximum communicative effectiveness, any fluency program sabotages itself by placing stress on correctness. Students simply cannot connect or develop ideas if they are preoccupied with spelling and grammar. Rather than generating and extending ideas, they get stuck on form. So any attention to correctness in the early stages of writing shuts down most writers' generative thinking.

---

*Some tricks I use to write a long journal is to write what I think on the topic and write it fast so I can get a lot done in the allotted time. I practice writing at home so I can write fast. Sometimes it's good to make a list about the topic and then explain everything on the list. The key is to not worry about spelling or grammar.*

---

—Joey Ma

At the same time, however, we also know that students need to take responsibility for the organization of their ideas, the complexity and variety of their syntax, and the accuracy of their spelling and punctuation. And (with a sigh) we know that students don't learn correctness in ways that are easy to understand. For some students, instruction in correctness seems to have no effect at all. They continue to make the same mistakes over and over. For others, there is no guarantee that spelling patterns taught are spelling patterns remembered. So if a journal program intends to improve students' overall literacy, it's got to address the conventions of writing. Where does correctness fit into our fluency program and what happens to student writing as a result?

First, though students are told from the earliest days of the *Rain, Steam, and Speed* program not to worry about spelling and grammar, certain features are built into the program to support correctness. You could call this "correctness scaffolding." You will find that the prompts are *wordy*—lots of words in lots of questions orbiting around a central idea. Students who are less confident writers or uncomfortable taking risks can simply appropriate the vocabulary from the prompts and answer the prompt questions. Other students can take words or ideas from the prompts as departure points and go off in their own directions, working with vocabulary and structures of their own. In this way, students are nudged out into the (sometimes) cold, cruel world of spontaneous writing with a host of vocabulary and structures from which to choose that are pristine in their correctness.

You yourself will read in detail later—and will witness—that once students internalize the template of the prompt, their fluency increases. And that significant improvement in their fluency is a vehicle toward correctness. Additionally, there's something to being attached to one's writing that "ratchets up" interest in the writing's being correct. Because the program is designed to tap students' interests and experiences, students assume ownership of their entries and become invested in the increased credibility of writing that is correct.

Finally, the gentle pushes and prods that the teacher gives through classroom monitoring during Journal Time, responding to oral reading, commenting on entries, and grading often indicate targets for correctness for individual students.

Indeed, correctness does improve. Students not only write more, they write better.

---

*My writing has taken a huge gigantic step up and forward. I feel like I have finally been relieved and I can succeed in all my work. I can really express myself through writing.*

---

—Alexander Thomas Ziv

## THE IMPORTANCE OF PROMPTS

In the same way that when one plants a fruit tree the original stock is of crucial importance in the flourishing of that new tree, the nature and elucidation of prompts is crucial to the flourishing of student writing. In working with emerging writers, we must understand that the writing prompt itself must be fluent if we're to expect our students' work to be fluent.

Deeper in that planted soil, the prompt itself must be germane to the lives of students: to their imaginations, their dreams, and their struggles. We'll discuss this further in Chapter Five, but be assured that the prompts provided in *Rain, Steam, and Speed* include those essential characteristics, and they *work* with students.

## MUSIC PROMOTES FLUENCY

Music plays a significant role in *Rain, Steam, and Speed.* You might already know of research claiming the positive effects of music study on the development of higher-order thinking skills, problem-solving ability, and increased motivation to learn. Additional evidence demonstrates that including music in the core curriculum provides access to a broad range of types of thinking. Howard Gardner's work on multiple intelligences shows us that learners with strengths in the musical spheres achieve at higher levels in all subjects when music is integrated into their studies. Likewise, auditory learners gain access to material when music becomes a key component of the curriculum. Therefore, in addition to the stimulus to delight, excite, and relax that the music component in *Rain, Steam, and Speed* provides, it also taps the thinking and learning preferences of more than the traditionally successful visual, linear learners.

Furthermore, the formal role of music in *Rain, Steam, and Speed* draws on the correlation between the structure of musical compositions and the organization of expository essays. Though structure is not explicitly taught in *Rain, Steam, and Speed,* it is implicitly presented through many of the music selections recommended in the Selected and Annotated Discography (Appendix A). The shape of a classical concerto and a straight-ahead jazz selection, for example, echo the organization of an expository essay. Traditional musical compositions that introduce an important idea, support the idea through variations in tempo, interval changes, and chord alterations, and finally come to a close with a recapitulation of the main idea reflect the structure and unity of a piece of academic writing—and listening to them imparts a gut-level understanding of that unity. The design of the prompts, with their series of questions that guide students to present main ideas and support and develop them through answers to specific questions, reinforces this organization.

Music in *Rain, Steam, and Speed* serves to broaden students' cultural horizons. The selections recommended in the discography present more than sixty CDs that feature music from many cultures and time periods. The instruments, tones, combinations of melodies, and rhythms that students encounter in *Rain, Steam, and Speed* are different from the music they listen to ordinarily. And students learn about and look forward to hearing more from recently discovered musicians.

Music is an important backbone of *Rain, Steam, and Speed* in one additional way. A critically important benefit of the music in this fluency development program (and the advantage most often cited by students) is its ability to help writers focus and develop ideas. Though it takes a short period of adjustment for some students, the integral addition of music to Journal Time becomes the key feature. We have included students' reflections on music throughout the book. Here is what eighth-grader Milo says:

*The music is helpful to me. I really like it. It helps me think and write. I usually don't write about a full page in twenty minutes. Usually it takes me about thirty minutes to write a full page. With the music on I can write more and more and it is really helping the creative process.*

—Milo Yee

## JOURNALS AND GENDER

One final preliminary comment before you learn the specifics of *Rain, Steam, and Speed*. For several years we have been following assessment results as they chronicle the steady performance gap between girls and boys in areas of literacy, with boys consistently performing at levels lower than their female counterparts. In *Reading Don't Fix No Chevys*, Michael Smith and Jeff Wilhelm report on a study they did with high school boys to find out what boys needed in order to be engaged. Among some other fascinating discoveries, they found that boys need to be in a condition of *flow* to sustain interest and motivation. Flow (easier for girls in school, generally) provides a sense of control and competence, challenge requiring an appropriate level of skill, clear goals and feedback, and a focus on immediate experiences.

In reviewing the journals from Jerry's classes, I looked carefully to see if girls outperformed boys, as they do on most literacy assignments. I found no gender gap on these journals. Boys who excelled did so at the same rate as girls; similarly, there were an equal number of weak journals from boys and girls. The explicit expectations, the achievable level of challenge, the stimulus of music, and the personal focus that are integral to the journals support all learners, and notably boys.

*As to the [music's] volume, I'd say, "The louder the better." That's because when I listen to my music, I'm used to having it to the max on the volume control. It just gives off a more lively feeling. Some might say it's distracting our work, but the last thing it does is distraction. It actually does the opposite.*

—Joey Ma

*Now I'm not embarrassed to write and I write faster and longer.*

—George Zhu

The conditions of flow are met here. Now I'll pass the narrative torch to Jerry, and you can embark on the joyful discovery ride of *Rain, Steam, and Speed.*

# PART ONE

# Rain

## Creating the Climate
## for Spontaneous Writing

# Introducing the Program to Students

You're about to embark upon a program that, if you choose to make it so, will last an entire school year and yield great results. As a teacher, though, you know well that you need to *lay the track,* so to speak—establish the climate for any sustained effort in a well-run classroom. Now we'll learn specific ways useful for establishing that climate, for allowing *Rain, Steam, and Speed* to take your students' writing where you want it to go.

## THE NITTY-GRITTY: MATERIALS YOU'LL NEED

We'll discuss rationale and step-by-step implementation at length later, but for now, here's what you'll need:

- The willingness to dedicate a total of thirty minutes a day, twice a week: no more, occasionally less.
- Simple $8\frac{1}{2} \times 11$-inch file folders for each student.
- Sixty pieces of binder paper for each student, to be parceled out in lots of twenty. It's preferable that all the binder paper be of the same stock.
- A big rubber band to hold the students' folders.
- A safe, out-of-sight place in the classroom to keep them.
- A decent-sounding—even if inexpensive—stereo system.

*—If all the paper all year is of the same stock size, kids can easily bind their journals at year-end. The binding can be as simple as yarn threaded through holes punched in the folders, or more elaborate. There's a sense of pride in assembling these formidable writings in May or June.*

- A small, soon-to-grow, collection of appropriate CDs.
- (For setup day) pens for kids who need them, crayons or felt markers, magazines to be cut up for collages, glue sticks, and scissors.

That's it. Pretty simple, pretty inexpensive.

## SETTING UP FOR SUCCESS: SELF-FULFILLING PROPHECIES

I've found it best to introduce the journal process in week four. Why begin in week four of a year? First, there's so much to do during those early weeks: getting to know the kids' names, passing out textbooks, dealing with the welter of paperwork, the frequent transition of students from class to class, and the frequent arrival of new kids to the school during those early times—these newcomers often the ones most needing the safe boundaries of our protocol. It's time-consuming to explain the journal process step-by-step to each individual new student who enters, so best wait a little.

As in any great gustatory experience or (yes!) lesson, anticipation is key. During the first two weeks of class, I keep anticipation high, saying, in various permutations twice each week or so:

> *And soon we'll be talking about our journals, which you'll see will be a very important part of this class. If you're like last year's class, you guys are really going to like this, and I just have a feeling that this particular class will do well.*

Such a mini-speech serves to heighten anticipation, of course, but also clearly creates a climate of self-fulfilling prophecy: you're establishing a sense of your own confidence in the class, and predicting payoff before they've even started. Good presenters know that promising to get to something soon and not delivering can

*—Have a student who enters mid-year? Take a trusted "veteran" aside and ask that student to explain the journal process to the new arrival. After the explanation, go over it quickly: OK, do you think you get the process? Any questions? Then, with its author's permission, of course, quickly show a journal whose quality you think is high.*

drive an audience first to distraction and then to anger, so just a few mentions of the journal during the first two or three weeks is enough.

During this chapter I'll continue to highlight the teacher monologue I use in my class during the critical days of introducing the Fluency Journals and their protocol. This is a dialogue that, through a kind of trial-and-error process, I find most successful—but your own voice is different, of course, and, though the elements are essential, this is not a script you have to follow for success.

## LAYING THE TRACK: THE FIRST DAYS

It's Tuesday of the fourth week: time to get rolling, time to pass out the folders. Again, anticipation is key.

> *OK, everybody. Remember we talked the other day about our journals? Well, today's the day you're making them your own. One of these for everyone.*

You distribute the folders personally: don't have a student pass them out.

Why not have a student pass them out? They will, later. But for today, these little folders are coming from the teacher's hand, conferring on them a little more importance.

> *Now: this is a really big project, everybody, and I want you to listen carefully.*
>
> *Today we're personalizing—decorating—our journals. We're going to do it in a couple of steps. First, I want you to right now write your name— your full name—in ink on the little tab that's sticking up. See the tab right here? Good. Write your name in ink, and right below that, write the period and Journal.*

You go to the board and write *Journal,* for there will be a few kids who don't know how to spell the word and don't want to admit it.

> *Raise hands when you've done that. Great. Now, for the rest of this period, I want you to make this journal your own—to personalize it by decorating it, front and back. This journal is going to be about your thoughts and feelings this year, your joys, your anger, your passion, so the way you decorate it should be about you—about who you are.*
>
> *If you're not a good artist, I don't care: just do a careful job on both sides. Can you draw crazy stuff? Sure. Can you do a collage? Yes: I've got magazines and glue sticks right over there. Help yourself. Can you write words on the front and back along with your pictures? Sure. Can you draw designs? Sure: I have a few rulers on the shelf, too, if you need them. Can you sit with somebody and talk while you're doing it? Yes, as long as you're working, and you finish by the period's end.*
>
> *Just remember: you'll be working with these twice a week, you'll be looking at them twice a week, I'll be taking them home to read, carrying them around, so make them really reflect who you are! Now let's get going.*

At least one student will raise a hand and ask, "Do I really have to do both sides? Can't I do just one?" The answer:

> *Nope: both sides.*

Dismiss any argument. (Why? You're raising the bar to begin with, requiring *more,* establishing a minor protocol in a process where protocol is crucial.)

However, do ask students not to either draw or write on the inside covers. You'll be using these for teacher comments later.

As the kids are drawing, you do two things: put some instrumental music on the stereo (full discussion of this to come), and go row by row parceling out your tall stack of binder paper, saying to the first student in each row,

> *Take twenty. Pass it back.*

> *—Twenty? the kids will say. Twenty, you'll reply, without elaboration. That bar is being raised again.*

Let's say the music you've chosen is Vivaldi's "Four Seasons." Some of the kids will express surprise, having never before heard music played in a classroom. Others will giggle at your "corny" choice. One might ask, "Can I put on my own CD?" to which you'll reply, *maybe another day, but only if it's instrumental.* Again, the foundation being built, inferentially.

For the rest of the period, then, students work making their folders their own. You might interrupt once, turning down the music to say:

> *There's some pretty great work going on in these folders—I like what I see!*

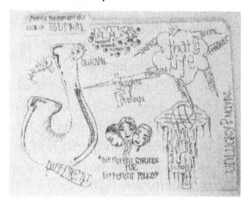

Then, later:

> *Only ten minutes left, everyone—let's finish these folders! We won't have time to work on them tomorrow!*

"Can we take them home to finish them?" some students will ask.

> *No, but I admire you for wanting to do that. Our journal folders stay at school.*

*—Students' motivation to take the folders home and work on them is admirable, and you should use your discretion in answer to this. My experience, though, is that some journals don't make it back, and the process starts all over for those students, bollixing up your timing, and some return in such ruin that the students themselves want to begin another. Better to keep them in your room, and you'll find that students will finish them, two minutes here and three minutes there, as the year goes on.*

## CHOOSING THE DISTRIBUTOR OF JOURNALS: END OF DAY ONE

Five minutes before the end of journal-personalizing day, you ask for the class's attention.

*I need to make a decision* [you say], *and I need to have your attention while I describe someone to you.*

*Someone needs to be in charge of passing out our journals every Tuesday and Thursday for the whole semester.* [Lots of hands go up.] *OK. Put your hands down for now, but thanks for volunteering. I need to describe this person, and as I describe this person, I want you to think about whether this description fits you.*

*First, I'm describing someone who hardly misses school. It's very rare that this person is absent, and this person is never tardy for class. Next, this person has to be trustworthy. What do I mean by trustworthy? I mean that this person would never read anyone else's journal. Never. Third, this person is self-motivated and has a good memory. He or she will come up to me at the very beginning of our Tuesday and Thursday class and ask, "Shall I pass out journals today?" And I'll usually say yes, and the person will go to the journal drawer and pass them out quickly and quietly. Finally, this person has a sense of decorum. What do I mean by decorum? Well, it's a kind of walking, talking dignity. For instance, when at the end of our twenty minutes this person collects the journals, you won't hear any chatting and giggling, the journals just get picked up. No big deal.*

*So: not absent much, on time, good memory, honorable, and low-key. Now: raise your hand if you think those criteria describe you. If you raise your hand, you're volunteering to be the Journal Passer-outer for the whole semester.*

Hands are raised, but relatively few. An interesting process of self-elimination has occurred; some names are called out in informal nomination by students whose hands are *not* raised, and those names are worth the teacher's attention—especially if the nominee has an upraised hand.

Choose a student, now, make it a little ceremonial, and thank the other volunteers, softening the rejection a little by suggesting that next semester they, too, may get a chance. Now, when the kids are back to work on their folders, go over and ask that student to come with you, show where the journals will be kept, and repeat the instructions briefly.

This seems like "small potatoes," but what we're building is a perception of ritual, and the miniature pageantry of this protocol helps make the journal program (rightly) seem *whole* to the kids.

## CLARIFYING THE CLASSROOM PROTOCOL (DAY TWO)

A full day has passed since the making of the journal folders themselves, and today, on this third day, you're ready for the big push. It's a very energetic day on your part—especially if you have multiple classes. You'll go home tired, but know that this was a day whose investment will pay off for many months—your payment coming in the currency of a steadily deepening curriculum, a solidifying community, and the tangible growth of your students' writing.

You gear up before class by assembling your simple props: a blank journal folder with a few pieces of binder paper in it, and a wide-nibbed felt-tip pen.

Let's call the student responsible for passing out the journals Maria. When Maria walks in, you whisper,

> *Maria—remember to pass out the journals today. OK?*

*Right away?* Maria will ask.

> *Yes—start now, if you would.*

Maria quietly passes out the journals while you're taking care of other class business.

*Are we going to do our journals today?* someone will ask.

> *We are—but I need to take roll and talk with you guys a little first.*

Actually, the talk today will be long. You take a deep, quiet breath and begin, circulating among the class as you talk.

> *OK, everybody. This is a really important day, so I need everyone's attention. Do you remember we've talked so much about how important our journals are going to be? Well, I need you to listen very carefully today, because right now I'm going to explain the process. And if you listen, you'll do better, and I won't have to repeat, and everyone will understand. Are you with me? Good. Here we go.*
>
> *All right. Now: you know that we'll be writing in our journals every Tuesday and Thursday, right?*

*—Choose whatever days work best in your class. For me, Mondays seem too hectic and interrupted, and often on Fridays the kids' energy flags, having been barraged with tests. So Tuesdays and Thursdays have worked best for me.*

---

*And you understand that the journals are important in terms of your grade, right? OK. So today we begin. But let's talk about the ground rules first—how we do our journals.*

*These are the rules. And if you have any questions, hang onto them until the end. I'll answer any questions you have at the end.*

*We write in our journals for twenty minutes, and Journal Time is quiet time. That means no talking. That means no talking. That means no talking at all—even if you're finished early (which will be rare) and one of your friends is finished early. No talking. No talking at all during the twenty minutes. It's about respect: respect for yourself, and respect for other writers focusing on their work. Everybody get that? Good.*

This may seem harsh now, perhaps, but you'll see its dividends later.

*What do we write about? Well, there are a number of possibilities. Every journal day I'll put a prompt, or a topic, on the board. Not just a few words as a prompt, but lots of words—I like to write, you know—and the prompt helps you write. We'll talk about that in a minute. So: you can write about the prompt on the board, or you can write on a subject of your own choosing.*

*Now: If you choose your own subject, what can you write about? That's up to you, and kids over the years have written about so many things. Some kids write about love, or death, or loneliness, or school, or arguments with their parents in the car on the way to school, or something they read, or what's going on in the world, ten thousand possible things. One student I had once started a story on the very first day of journal and kept writing it for the entire year. It ended up being a novel, really—it was that fat— and I admit that by January I kind of lost track of the story line: he had about fourteen million main characters, there were swords and lightning bolts and magicians, and I just couldn't keep the players straight, there were so many of them. But he loved it, and he loved writing in it, and I loved that he loved writing in it. And his sentences and paragraphs got better as the weeks went on!*

*Journal Time is a time to be yourself—to review your actions, character, ideas, thoughts, dreams, wishes. It gives you the rare opportunity to figure yourself out.*

—Charles Kwan

*If you've got something troubling you, you should really try to put it down on paper. Why does it confuse you? Ask questions, and though you may not know how to answer them, try to think of possible replies, then write them down. Write down what you think should be done about the matter.*

—Christine Lee

*So you can write what you want. Only very rarely will the prompt on the board be mandatory. (Who can tell the class what mandatory means? Good. Right. Compulsory is another word for mandatory.) And if a prompt*

*—Prompts in this book will generate anywhere from a 60 to 90 percent choose-the-teacher's-prompt rate—usually toward the higher end.*

*is mandatory for that day, I'll be sure to let you know. But this will only happen three or four times a year.*

*Got it? Great. So you understand that you don't have to write on the prompt, though lots of kids do, because they often like the prompts. So: let's say you write using one of your own ideas, or what's on your mind. Let me ask you this. If you decide to write on your own topic, please don't give me this:*

*I got up at 7:30. I ate breakfast. I came downstairs. The dog was still sleeping. I ran to get the bus, then got to school just in time.*

*Then, the next day we do journals, the same student writes:*

*I got up at 7:31. I ate breakfast. I was hungry, and ate so much I missed my bus. Too bad I was late to school.*

The kids will laugh here: capitalize on the laughter's energy in your transition toward describing the power of kids' volition in the possibilities of *depth* in journal.

*No! For goodness sake, that's not what I'm looking for! Not only is it way too short, but it's simply a recapitulation of what this kid's <u>body</u> does every day. That might be a little interesting, but these journals are about what you think about things and about what you feel in here—in your heart. And they're about taking new chances in your writing, they're about saying things you've never said before! These journals are for you, finally, because at the end of the year you'll be taking them home, and one year in the distant or not-so-distant future you'll look back and say, "Aha! That's who I was in that grade! I had those ideas even then!" And you'll be proud of your writing. See what I'm saying? See the difference between the two types of journals? I hope so.*

## ADDRESSING PRIVACY AND CHILD ABUSE ISSUES

Your monologue continues:

*One more thing about writing what you want. Sometimes you might want it to be private. Now we all know that kids never read each other's journals unless they have the owner's permission, right? And we know that they're kept safely in the filing cabinet. But sometimes maybe you're not too crazy about the idea of <u>me</u> reading what you write.*

*Well, in that case, there's something you can do. Take your pen and draw a fence around your writing, like this:* [The teacher takes the felt-tip pen and sketches out a primitive "fence" around the inside perimeter of a piece of binder paper, holds it up for the class.]

*All right, I know: it's not beautiful. But you get the point. And now you write "Private" all around the fence.* [Teacher scribbles "Private" a few times around perimeter of the "fence."]

*What does that mean? Well, that means that I'll only scan it for length—how long your writing is—and we'll talk more about the length of your writing in a minute—and I'll scan it for danger. What do I mean by danger?*

*Here's what I mean. Did you know that it's a law that a teacher who is aware of any form of child abuse happening to any of his students absolutely must report it? Well, that's true. And I want two things for you: I want you to feel as if you can write freely in your journal, but I also want you to be safe in this class and in your life. It's part of my job to make sure you're safe. So here's what I do: I skim the private entries—the entries you put a fence around. To skim means to read fast. So I skim them for length and to see quickly if my "worry bell" goes off.*

*Most of the time my worry bell doesn't go off. Most of the time your "private" entries will be boyfriend or girlfriend stuff, "She dumped me!" "He dumped me!"* [The kids will laugh here.] *And maybe about arguments with parents or worries about school—all very normal stuff for kids your age. But you need to know that when you write your "private" entries I will be glancing at them very quickly. And you also need to know that I never talk to other kids about what you have written in your journal. It's none of their business, and I feel lucky that you share your thoughts with the paper and with me!*

*But I need to tell you clearly: if it does occur that I see evidence of child abuse in any form in a journal, it's my job to report it. I have to do that, and I want to do that—it really helps the kid.*

Often students will ask, "Have you ever read about any child abuse in the journals?" This is a prime opportunity to solidify their feeling that they can be free to write what they *need* to write. If asked, I will tell them about a girl in my class a few years ago who was being abused by an uncle. "I don't want to go into the details," I'll say, and let the kids know that it was very brave of the girl to write about it in her journal and that we were able to get her help immediately. I'll often volunteer this incident even if kids don't ask, for I believe strongly that students who may be in trouble *need* that entrée toward help. You will get such journal entries, and do follow the law assiduously in reporting them. It's not at all an issue of *whether*.

One student in my class reported in a "private" journal entry that when he and his brother arrived at home after school, their father had them stand in a corner with their arms in the air until dinner time. We did a Child Protective Services report, and the father and the family went into counseling. I ran into that student on a San Francisco street some years ago—a big guy, then in his twenties—and he thanked me for that intervention. "My dad was just trying to get us to be disciplined," he said, "and he just didn't know how to do it."

The pep talk continues:

> *Two more things about this privacy issue. First, please don't do thirty thousand "private" entries that I won't be able to read! A few of them would be fine, but I want to get to know you and your writing during this process, and if I can't get in there to read them, how will I know you and help you in your writing? So use your "private" prerogative judiciously— just a few, OK?*
>
> *Last thing about privacy. I take the journals home toward the end of the quarter, I sit down on my couch, and I read and read. But I do wait until near the end of the quarter. So if for some reason you want me to read your journal right away—for any reason, even if you think it's silly or you just want to ask me a question—or if there's a more serious reason—when Maria quietly comes around to collect the journal, just say to her, "I'm keeping mine," and she'll walk right past you. OK, Maria? She won't say,*

> *—There won't be many "private" entries at first, of course. But as the year progresses and the kids become more trusting of you, you'll see quite a few.*

*"Oh, you're keeping your journal, eh?" Not a word: she'll just keep collecting the rest of the journals and put them away. Then, at the end of class, just put your journal on top of my desk, and on the way out say, "Mr. Fleming, I put my journal on your desk." And that will be my signal to read it just as soon as I get a minute—and that will be very soon.*

When a student *does* do that—and it happens frequently—I make sure to read it immediately, even if it means altering the activities of the first few minutes of my next class slightly.

To continue:

*Does everybody understand that? Who can repeat for the class what to do if you want me to read your journal right away?*

A student raises a hand and accurately summarizes what you've just said.

## EXPLAINING THE GRADING CRITERIA

You continue:

*OK, folks. Now comes the wonderful part. You're going to love this. How are these journals graded? Here we go.* [The teacher gets quite dramatic here, takes from the folder a blank piece of binder paper, wields again the dark felt-tipped pen.] *If, on average over the quarter, you write THIS much* ... [The teacher takes the felt tip pen and strokes lines on the paper, those dark lines filling half of the front side of the paper. Shows it around.] *Remember, on average, that is ... you will receive a "C" in your journal.*

There's a gasp, and a few underbreath complaints. But the teacher doesn't respond, and continues:

*AND IF, over the quarter, you write, AGAIN, ON AVERAGE—and remember, ON AVERAGE means that you might write a little more one day and a little less another day—so if you average about THIS much* ... [The teacher takes the pen and now fills the entirety of the front page.] *That will get you a "B."*

More gasps, the students having expected you to say "A."

*—This option—to have the teacher read a journal immediately—was born the day after I did a journal-writing workshop in a tough urban district in Southern California. We were talking about privacy in journals, and a teacher—clearly, still in grief—raised her hand and related the story of one of her students who had committed suicide the year before. This teacher, too, took her journals home for review only every nine weeks or so. The teacher, upon reading the girl's journal after her tragic death, discovered that she'd threatened suicide in that very journal, and it hadn't been read. Of course, the teacher's story stunned our little workshop group, and compelled us to come up with ways in which a student could, via some imperative, have a teacher look at the journal immediately. What I've described here seemed the best way and has worked very well for me over the years. (Thankfully, few "read this immediately" requests reflect such life-or-death seriousness: most are friendly banter, questions about whether or not I watched a particular sit-com the night before, and so on. But occasionally they're quite serious and need to be acted upon post haste. But any journal process, it seems, must include this "alarm button." (Similarly, if I notice that someone seems depressed more than a day or so, I'll pull that student's journal prematurely to see if there's a problem, or if there's anything I might be able to help with. Such caution is worth thirty seconds in a long day's time.)*

---

*And finally, if you write, again, ON AVERAGE, this much—and you'll be surprised, you guys—you'll be able to write much more than you thought!—if you write this much ...* [The teacher flips the paper now, and strokes out five or six thick lines on the back of the same paper.] *You'll get an "A." And I will give "A" pluses to anyone who consistently writes more than that!*

The students are a little stunned, and an instant demoralization settles in among the crowd.

*OK, I feel you guys getting a little nervous now, so I want to let you know some things I'm not going to worry about. The first is spelling.*

Remember that this is timed writing, so I don't want you to have to take up your valuable time going to the dictionary, stressing over how to spell a word. Just spell it as well as you can and move on.

The second thing I'm not going to worry about too much at this point is grammar. Again, if you're stressed out over whether a sentence is grammatical, you're losing time—time I'd rather see you use in thinking and writing—and you'll end up with very little writing by the end of the twenty minutes. See?

So: Am I going to be counting spelling errors against you?

If you've gotten your point across, you'll get a chorus of "No."

And am I going to be worrying about the correctness of your grammar?

Again, the "No" chorus.

---

*Personally, I really enjoy doing the journal writing. I think it has improved my writing a lot. I've found that I can easily write a page about mostly anything. So, when those essays for the High School Exit Exam come around, I won't have any trouble with them. Doing the journal has improved my grammar and vocabulary as well. When I'm writing I'm learning more about punctuation and stuff like that. I also get a chance to use new words I have learned. In other words, the journal writing is very helpful to me.*

---

—Alison Gaik

OK—good. You got it. Now, though, I want to let you know about some things I do worry about.

First: If you choose the prompt on the board, I want you to stay on the topic and not jump around to another topic. For example, I don't want *you to say, "Yes, I think I know what love is"—then you write a paragraph about love, and continue, in the next paragraph, "And by the way, I saw an accident on my way to school today. This guy ran a red light, and. . . ." No: If you're with a topic—whether it's the love prompt that I put on the board or another topic you want to write about—stay with it.*

*Now that doesn't mean your mind can't jump around into smaller or larger topics inside that topic—do you know what I mean? It can, as long as you're still writing about the central topic.*

This is a good opportunity to remind the kids about paragraph breaks, very briefly. I like to say two things about paragraphing: The first is that paragraphing is like driving a stick-shift car—the whole piece of writing is going in the same direction, but just needs to shift gears once in a while. The second is to reinforce the idea that if a student has an instinct that it might be time to start a new paragraph, that instinct is almost always right.

*OK, so stay on topic. By the way—whatever topic you choose, please be sure to put a little title and a date on the first line. You'll need to arrange your journals by date, so that's why the date's important. And I need a title to figure out what you're writing about. But don't fuss over beautiful titles. Wait until you're finished writing—then you know what it really was about. Then go back and put a few words on the top line as a title to give me a key into the door of your writing, OK? Otherwise, when I read it, it takes me a paragraph to figure out what you're writing about!*

---

*It's good to have a central idea that you can go back to every time you get stuck. Usually that central idea is your title. It's good that way because you can look at your paper and see that title and you go, "Oh yeah, that's what I'm writing about."*

---

—Celia Kitchell

*Next, neatness. First, I want you to write in pen. Pen is more dignified, and this journal will be something you'll want to look at in many years. And when you're using pen, you're not thinking about erasing, which would waste your valuable time. And regarding pen, please use dark blue or black ink in your journal—if you don't have that today, it's OK, but next time, please have a dark blue or black pen.*

One student will ask, "Why?"

*Why a dark blue or black pen? Well, over the years I've had students write in yellow pen, pink pen, all kinds of colors. They're impossible to read! Have you ever tried reading five paragraphs in yellow pen? You go crazy!*

*Finally, a little warning. There are kids who think they can "beat the system" by writing FIVE words on a line* [the teacher scribbles five words on a line of blank paper, then five words on the next] *and FIVE words on the next, and hope to get a decent grade. NOPE. I'm onto the trick, you guys.* [Laughter.] *That's an old trick, and don't even try it!* [The teacher laughs in a creepy Bella Lugosi imitation.]

*And there's another old trick: fat margins!* [Drama's increasing here, humor in the room.] *This student writes five or six words and there are these margins on the right side that you can sail a ship through. Nope.*

*Here's the rule on margins in your journal. Is everybody listening? I want you to take a piece of paper from your journal, and put your thumb pointing upward on the right side of a piece of paper. That's right: put your thumb there, and let me see. OK, good. That's the size of the margin I want in these journals—the size of your thumb. Not two thumbs, not three, but one of your wonderful, opposable thumbs.*

*Does everybody get that? So, how big a margin should be on the right side? That's right: a thumb's width. Good.*

*Oops, one more thing, now that we're talking about thumbs. You'll be writing a lot of paragraphs here, right?*

*Students agree, if grudgingly.*

*—This lesson on my part was learned the hard way. Imagine trying to run a "silent" journal session in a class of thirty-five kids pushing pencils across the page; four kids at any given moment need to sharpen theirs. Imagine trying to read page after page of thirty-five journals in the near-phantom image pencils often create. Imagine that yellow ink, that pink, your eyes at the end of the day . . . you get the picture.*

*So here's the rule for paragraphing: please indent by only the width of one thumb. Not length, but width. See? One thumb, that's all: no indents that sink deep into the page like deep-sea divers—one thumb only.*

A student may raise a hand and say, "But I'm not used to that! I indent a lot!" To which you reply, *Fine. Indent a little more, if you want, in* other *papers you hand in to me. But in journals, just remember:* one thumb only.

## INTRODUCING THE MUSIC COMPONENT

We're getting close to the end of the orientation now, and push on:

*One more thing I should mention. During the twenty minutes of journal, I'll be playing music. The music will be fairly loud, and that might be strange for you at first, but you'll get used to it, and after a few sessions you'll like the volume.*

*The music I play will mostly be instrumental—can anyone explain what instrumental means?—yes, that's right, only instruments, no singing—and it will be of all different types: classical, jazz, world music, lots of different pieces.*

A student may ask, "Can we bring our own music in?"

*Can you bring your own music in? Sure, as the year gets going a little. But it has to be instrumental, and I'd have to listen to it first. But yes, sure, we can do that once in a while.*

*The first time that Mr. Fleming turned on music during journal, I thought it was distracting, to tell you the truth. But after we finished the journal for that day, I realized not only was the music not distracting, it helped me write more than I've ever written in twenty minutes. Sure, I might have one or two spelling errors, but after a person writes that much in so little time, it makes them feel better. It boosts them into believing in themselves more often.*

—Andrea Chan

## REVIEWING THE PROTOCOL

This little oral review is important.

*All right: This has been really long, and your attention has been great, everyone. So let's go over what you've just learned about how we do our journals.*

*How many days a week will we being doing journal? That's right, two.*

*How long do we have to write each day? Yup: twenty minutes.*

*Can we talk during Journal Time? Nope. Never. That's right. If you're finished early, you're reading a book. Please always have a book to read in case you finish early.*

*Can you write about anything you want? Sure: and if it's private, remember to draw that fence.*

*How are you graded? Right: half a page on average gets you a "C," full front side gets you a "B," and consistently going to the back side gets you an "A." By the way, did I mention this? It is very possible to get an "A+" in journal! And again, remember, we're doing this twice a week and taking a lot of class time, so this counts heavily on your grade—take it seriously!*

*Do we use a new piece of paper for every new day? Yes, a new piece of paper for each new journal entry.*

This is new information, but it's the best place to put it in. (It's much easier for the teacher to evaluate the journals if each entry is on a separate piece of paper.)

> *Am I worried about spelling? Nope, but of course, spell as well as you can.*
>
> *Am I stressing grammar here? Nope. But would I like it if you write some fancy sentences, and use adjectives, and write passionately or persuasively? Sure!*
>
> *OK. Now, let's say you've got something "hot," or something you're worried about and you want me to read your journal right away: What do you do?*
>
> *That's right. Tell Maria you're keeping it, put it on my desk on the way out, and be sure to let me know that it's on my desk. Good.*
>
> *All right—we're ready to begin our journals! But let me ask a question first: How many kids at this point feel overwhelmed?*

Lots of hands will go up.

> *Well, I understand. I really do. And it's hard for you to know this now, but the whole process really goes smoothly once you get the hang of it. And you'll get the hang of it very quickly. Really. Take my word for it: you'll do fine.*
>
> *Aha: I see we only have fifteen minutes left. We'll read the prompt, and that will take about five minutes, so right now I want you to put today's date on the far right side of the first line. Raise your hands when you've done that. Now, at the very top, I want you to write "Ten Minutes Today," so I'll remember that you guys only had ten minutes because of today's orientation. Did you do that? Great. Now we're ready to read the prompt.*

## PRESENTING THE FIRST PROMPT

When the kids arrive in class, your most visible chalkboard or whiteboard is already full with today's prompt. Prompts take about five minutes to put up and are impressive to the kids: the entire board is filled with *your* handwriting, *your* labor.

On the first day, I usually have a prompt on the subject of *journals* on the board. It may indeed be the driest prompt of the year, but its topicality is important, for it intensifies the day's inculcation into the journal process and gives kids a chance to express their opinions on what they've heard so far. (See full discussion on the nature and rationale for prompts in Chapter Five.)

*—The teacher doesn't title the prompts on the board. That undercuts kids' own developing titling skills and imposes upon kids what we adults believe the topic is "about." They may see something different in it.*

**The first day's prompt** looks something like this:

> *Have you written in journals before, either at home or in school?*
> *What was the nature of your writing: was it on particular subjects, or was it simply "freewrites," wherein you wrote what you felt like writing?*
> *If you had journals in school, how did the teacher structure them? Were you satisfied with the process? Did you feel as if you did well, or were you unsatisfied?*
> *And what about this journal process this year? Are you feeling a little overwhelmed, or are you confident? Are you eager to write about lots of things, or are you anxious (nervous)?*
> *Write about journals today.*

Yes, this one's dry, but when kids later look back on early expressions of trepidation in response to this prompt, they're proud of the distance they've come as writers.

I've found it effective to introduce *all prompts* in a particular way, having learned that it's not wise to assume that students can read my handwriting, or can or will read the entire prompt, getting its theme and subtleties, its questions and triggers.

Here's what I say:

> *OK, everybody, let's take a look at the prompt. Is there anyone who'd like to read it out loud?*

A few kids raise their hands. Choose someone whose oral reading skills you know are fairly sophisticated.

> *Great, Steven, thanks. Take a try at reading that handwriting of mine to the class.*

*I think what helps me is the music. It's never too loud and it's very calming. Although it isn't my favorite choice in music, it helps me center my thoughts. It helps me bring things to my mind that I have never realized I've known before.*

—Tiffany Hackley

Steven begins reading the prompt, and you help him along if he falters. He gets to the end, and you thank him sincerely, perhaps in admiration of his bravery in deciphering your cursive. *Then you rephrase the prompt:*

> *So what is this journal about? It's about journals themselves. I'm wanting to know whether you've written journals before, where, how you like them, what subjects you wrote on, whether you felt you did well. And I'm interested in how you're feeling about this journal protocol in this class. Are you feeling overwhelmed?* [Yes! some kids answer.] *OK, then, if you are, write about it and tell why. But maybe you're feeling excited and eager. Write about that, too.*
>
> *Everybody get it?*
>
> *One more thing: Do you have to write about this?*

"No!" the kids say.

> *That's right! This is not mandatory.*
>
> *All right, everybody. Quiet time, Journal Time: you're writing now for the next, let's see, ten minutes. It's a short entry, but let's get going.*

If you've delivered your journal explanation in the way described here, you have pretty close to ten minutes left in today's fifty-minute period. That's great, for a ten-minute writing session is kinder to kids who feel as if they might have a hard time in this project, and the short time serves to whet the whistle for those whose writing voices are eager to trill their tune.

The kids begin writing, and you go to the stereo and put on your first piece of music: a quiet piece today, at relatively low volume.

## Journal Day Routine

- Teacher writes prompt on the board before class begins.
- Student monitor passes out journals immediately.
- Teacher chooses a student to read the prompt aloud.
- Student reads the prompt.
- Teacher reviews and rewords prompt for kids, checks for understanding.
- "Journal Time—quiet time!"
- Writing begins.
- Teacher puts on music.
- Teacher gives a little warning before the end: "Two more minutes, everybody!"
- Time to stop—twenty minutes (or thereabouts) is up.
- Student collects journals, returns them to cabinet.
- Optional oral reading of journals: volunteers.

# The Essential Role of Music

*When I am exposed to music during the process of
writing, my mind opens wide and gives me a variety
of choices for writing. The music gives me many
ideas and wraps me into writing—completely. If the
volume were louder, it would be even better because
it makes me feel as if I were actually there in the
place where the musicians are playing the music.*

*The music gives me different images, which
form in my head and tell me what writing structure
I should use. I know, it seems completely crazy, but it
just does. The images support the way I am thinking
and especially the way I am writing. The music gives
different topics and somehow seems to beg me to
write about them. It's fantastic.*

—Lisa Nip

So we've set the climate. The kids are clear on what to expect. Now, Rain—the steady rain of good music—will sustain the Fluency Journals, week to week, month to month, until that late spring day when you say, "Well, everyone, this will be our last journal entry of the year," and the kids sigh a little—a few in relief, but most in a minor grief, for they know they'll soon miss what the program represented for them.

What will it have represented to them? A time spent with self, a time in which not only their writing—self-driven in its subject matter, guided when they wanted by the prompts—flourished. It also will have been a time in which they were exposed to music they've never heard: music whose range might well open for them entirely new aural worlds, now or later.

We'll talk more about the nature of the music to which I hope you'll consider exposing students, but first a twofold insistence, each fold sheltered inside the rationale Meredith offered in Chapter Two.

Here's the first fold: Whatever music you play during Journal Time, make it the best of its kind—a strong example of its genre; its players, either living or dead, recognized as masters in their field. (The book you're reading quivers at the prospect of Fluency Journals being accompanied by a rain of Kenny G. or Yanni or any New-Age relaxation music, and contains a built-in self-destruct mechanism that will melt away its words into an inky puddle of sentimental tears should such a crime against the human ear occur.)

---

*All these famous musicians' playing really inspires
me to write more in my journals.*

---

—Darrell Chan

The second fold: Please understand that the Steam (teacher prompts or student-selected topics) and the Speed (protocol and timed writing) will serve well for just two months without the Rain of accompanying music. Really, that's all you'll get: two rather uneven months.

The music accompanying the twenty minutes of journal, and its attendant volume, functions on many levels—not simply as diversion. If it's interesting enough, it certainly does divert—not away from writing, as in distraction, as some might suspect, but toward new direction and license in writing. Great music springs us loose from the constraints of our lives, from petty worries or troubles looming large. Great music in its unexpected turns takes us along with it, great train on its frontierward tracks, as listeners and as writers. Great music brings us alive, widens the self, plays not only with our emotions (any sentimental claptrap can do that) but also, simultaneously, with our intellect. When years ago I began the journal process, I put on music in an effort to "relax" kids. I didn't expect to learn that they'd write more—and more vividly—as the quality and complexity and range of the music I offered widened and intensified.

> *I take advantage of the music. Instead of annoying*
> *pens and pencils tapping on the table, we get nice*
> *music. It may also help create ideas, like when a*
> *melody comes into your head.*

> —Benita Cruz

Music during Journal Time serves another role, and this is where the "No Music = Two Months Maximum" axiom comes in.

I've discovered that, after the first few (musically quieter) introductory sessions of Journal Time, turning the volume up on my stereo to a level that kids are accustomed to in wearing headsets but not accustomed to in a classroom setting has another powerful function: it serves as Class Manager: an efficient, if wordless, disciplinarian.

How can that be?

Have you ever tried talking with someone at the end of a film when the credits are rolling and the theme music is playing at high volume? Or tried talking with a friend sitting beside you in a small music club while musicians play? It's tough to do, and after a few tries, you give up, saving your talk until after the music's over.

So it is when kids are writing intensively for twenty minutes, when they're interested in the prompt, when new, interesting, or at least oddly provocative music is on the stereo, and a talkative neighbor tries to get a few words in. It's a bother, it's difficult to hear and be heard, and ultimately not worth the effort.

No, your music needn't blare nor shake the walls, disturbing the entire school, but it should be at a volume that, if your doors were open, would easily be heard in the hall. (Worried about disturbing the classes next door, I attached some inexpensive adhesive-backed foam weather stripping to the insides of my classroom doorjambs. My teacher friends next door, east and west, have remained friends, and claim they can't hear the music during Journal Time.)

## NECESSARY EQUIPMENT

Not much is called for. Here's what I have in my classroom: an inexpensive receiver (the PTA bought it for me), a *very* inexpensive portable CD player (bought used from a student who'd just gotten a newer one), and four speakers, strategically placed on walls around the classroom, each pair bought for a few dollars at a garage sale. Setting the whole system up in the classroom took me a couple of hours, but it's been up for many years now, and that minor labor's long behind me.

How would the system be rated by an audiophile? Not highly, certainly, but the speakers are capable of adequate treble and bass to do justice to the music, and the amplifier is capable of sufficient volume.

Some of the boom boxes on the market today are both inexpensive and of remarkably faithful sound quality. (If I were to bring in one of those, I'd want to make sure that I was able to detach and separate the speakers so that the benefit of stereo sound would be available. Some recordings sound so great on stereo, and the kids are thrilled by them. If speakers are widely separated, students on one side of the room aren't blasted with sound while others go wanting.)

## SELECTION AND PROGRESSION OF MUSIC

First, it's clear that the music must be instrumental. I experimented briefly with music containing English or Spanish lyrics, and learned quickly that kids, not surprisingly, have a very hard time writing when recognizable words are circulating in the air around them. (However, strangely, I've also found that if the music is in a language that no one in the class understands—say, Latin Gregorian chants or Bulgarian choruses—the kids do well. So once in a while, after the journal process is well established, I'll sneak in one of those.) Appendix A provides an annotated discography representing music that works well in the Fluency Journal process.

It seems important that during the sweep of a school year kids experience a range of music that includes classical, contemporary composers, jazz, bluegrass, a little fusion, and world music. Similarly, recordings should reflect both virtuoso solo performances—the exultant miracle of individual perfectibility—and group orchestral performances, wherein the class can witness the magic of human collaboration.

---

*The music you play interests me a lot. Especially the Bali music. It's such a pleasant sound. Reminds me of Vietnam, since it is from Asia. Some other songs I never even heard before too, which is great, because I could open myself to other kinds of music other than rap, hip hop, and R & B. If you didn't play music when I do journal entries, I would absolutely hate it. It would be so boring. The class would be so silent which is a bit scary. Without the music I would hate doing journal entries. Well that's just what I think.*

---

—Lynn Huynh

Is there a preferred progression, genre to genre? I don't think so.

Some years I've had fun playing only classical music during the fall semester: begin with early, pre-Baroque music, progressing through the centuries, ending the fall with Gershwin through Vaughn Williams through Steve Reich and Philip Glass and Lou Harrison. Then, in spring, jazz—again in progression, including Joplin and New Orleans through, say, Bechet and Miles and Monk, Oscar Peterson and Wynton Marsalis; then world music: Cuban and Venezuelan and Chinese and Balinese and Pygmy chants and even goofy German calliope.

Other years I let whim inform me and tend to play random selections, most often based on the nature of the prompt, but occasionally based on either my mood or the mood it seems the kids are in. (Clearly, occasionally the kids are in a mood that signals *No Wild Music Today, Teacher!* For that reason, I've included a

"Frenetic Scale" in the discography so that teachers can gauge the antic index of particular selections.)

Two quick notes, so to speak. For the first few journal sessions, I tend to play slower, rather patterned pieces: the rhythmics and mathematics of Bach piano, for example, or of Satie, each at only moderate volume. After six or so sessions, the volume gradually goes up, and the music becomes more complex and polyrhythmic. The kids are in the swing of the protocol now and can tolerate the stimulus. The "Frenetic Scale" for each CD can be useful when you're thinking about timing of pieces during the school year. I reserve music very high on the "Frenetic Scale" for the second semester, when the journal process is second nature, and most protocol issues have been resolved, either individually or classwide. Powerful, impressive music can therefore make its way into second-semester writing, and results can be spectacular, astonishing.

Speaking of stimulus, a final note: the intention of this Rain—this music—is *not* relaxation; for though once in a while we may want to calm kids down—and music can create that meditative state—an entire semester of calming music would be deadly wearisome to the kids. We want their synapses firing, not dozing, and writing itself cannot catch fire if the brain that ignites it is numbed and enervated by week after week of listless (Lisztless? Think *Hungarian Rhapsodies*) synthesizer robotics or New-Age treacle.

Good music, much of it new to the kids' ears, creates a sense of dynamic tension. You'll notice that a kind of triangulation occurs: the familiarity and comfort of the journal routine as one side, the interest and energy elicited by the prompt as the second, and the unfamiliar and emotionally stimulating music as the third. It's a joy for a teacher to see the triangle of that dynamic tension at work, generating, creating, and to witness its product: truly interesting writing.

---

*What do I like about Journal Time? I like Journal
Time because you can think about your thoughts
more! I like Journal Time because when the music is
on, you can think more!*

---

—Stella Chin

## LETTING STUDENTS KNOW WHAT'S PLAYING

Kids are so honest in what they need; if you're listening, they'll tell you.

Two years into the study of what music works for kids in Fluency Journals, I introduced a prompt, and before students began writing, a girl who rarely raised her hand tentatively poked a few fingers into the air.

"Mr. Fleming, why don't you ever tell us what music you're playing?"

I couldn't answer, except to apologize for my rudeness: I'd put lots of energy into choosing music for the project, but hadn't been polite enough to let kids know whose notes surrounded them for twenty minutes each Tuesday and Thursday.

An easy fix: a trip to an office supply store and the purchase of a small whiteboard that I attached to the wall, on which I simply wrote *Now Playing*, and on which I fill in the day's selection. It only takes a minute, and its results have been interesting. For a while I didn't think kids were looking at it, but soon I overheard kids saying the musician's name. (And Keane, one day saying to me, "Hey, Mr. Fleming—got any more of that Philip Glass stuff?")

**PART TWO**

# Steam

## Prompts for Inspiration

# Focusing on Topics That Matter

The evolution of the Fluency Journal prompts has been a gradual one for me—a process full of surprise and discovery.

Whereas in the beginning of my own development as a teacher I was certain that the more open-ended a prompt was, the more energized a student's writing would be, I've moved toward the other pole of that thinking. Remembering that kids have the option to write on the prompt, on a topic of their own choice, or on a topic they began earlier, I've discovered that in prompts kids want more direction, not less. It does students a disservice to put a single sentence on the board: "What is your favorite sport, and why?" Any sane person would blank out at such a lethargic and undeveloped question.

*Journals are much easier to write if there are more details in the question.*

—Amy Lin

As teachers, we have a responsibility to assume prior experience on students' parts, but I don't think we ought to assume specific prior knowledge. Knowledge of the structure of a well-developed piece of writing, for example, is neither inherited nor intuited. It's learned, and by the time you and I get to the place we are today—you reading these words, I writing them—we've accumulated layer upon layer of knowledge: some of those layers discrete, some woven together so tightly they seem as one. That knowledge includes conventions, the decorum of standard English, and skill after skill, subtlety after rhetorical subtlety learned and relearned.

If I asked you now to write for twenty minutes on the nature of love, for example, an entire "template"—not only of experience, but also of assertion and argument and speculation—would snap into place in your brain. You'd start out, perhaps, with a bold or general statement, move to specifics, then end, even tentatively, with a rephrased but strengthened, assertion.

But we can't assume that kids have mastered such little jigsaw-pieces of inculcation: this conditioning is so deep we take it for granted. And we can't assume that kids' minds have yet arrived at even the questions to ask reflexively or reflectively while writing extended prose, much less the answers to those questions.

So what do we do? We supply the pattern, and supply it so regularly that by the end of the school year it becomes second nature to the student writer, an instant extrapolation template that can be lowered into place on demand. *Clank.*

We don't, therefore, write a measly, emaciated sentence on the board and expect kids to spontaneously generate a few hundred words on the core idea contained therein—a core idea safely locked inside the *teacher's* mind.

We do the opposite: establish a subject that kids *are* (not "should be") interested in, ask a question, and sketch out possible implications and complications to that question by asking further questions inside the larger question. We keep the prose lively and interesting, we invest a little energy, and we fill the board with a fully developed prompt.

What's the effect of this?

First, kids come into the classroom and see that *you,* the teacher, have used some of your time that morning moving your body one side to the other of the chalkboard in the service of *their* writing development. They see the effort you've put into the words that are on the board. They infer, rightly, that you're interested in the subject about which you'll be asking them to write. They see that you, the teacher, can write, have been writing, and now ask them to do the same. (For the first few days, you'll notice that kids marvel at that chalkboard full of your writing.)

Second, the prompt's depth or imaginative specificity offers students a structure from which their thoughts can spring. Those thoughts begin on the track you've laid down, then take their own individual course.

*I think it is very hard to write but I stop for a minute and think about what I'm going to write and I come up with a lot of stuff to say. I write it down and it's very long so I stop and read it over. Then I start to write again.*

—Nate Fullard

Third, the prompt's specificity offers them—especially recalcitrant writers—real questions on which they can hang paragraphs.

As the weeks go on I identify kids who are having trouble, and I'll confer with them briefly, suggesting, "Do you notice how there are quite a few questions and those little wonderings out loud in the prompts, Marlon? Well, if you just took those questions one by one and wrote a paragraph in response to each one, before you knew it, you'd have a really long piece of writing!" Marlon tries it, and sure enough, it works.

Finally, students recognize and come to respect your fearlessness. They see that, by the nature of your prompts, you don't shy away from the tough issues: love, death, anger, joy, teenage issues with parents and peers, and other serious topics central to our lives. (Well, near-fearlessness. Our residual Puritanism still doesn't allow for frank discussion of sex.) They see that, in offering such topics, you respect their minds; you assume that they have thoughts and feelings on the issues with which we humans struggle.

It is this sense of *struggle for truth*, elusive as truth's definition might be, that interests them. You can assume that few teachers in the past have asked them to write in an extended way on such core *(coeur?)* matters. And we must assume that kids do contemplate, often, the same matters that trouble us and engage our minds as adults. Further, if we assume that they do consider these things but process them in a more primitive way, we're making a huge mistake. I've learned much from student journals, and each time I come away from a journal-reading session I feel faith in the world's future. Even young adolescents process complex ideas in extremely sophisticated ways, often with a perspective and profundity absent in many (voting!) adults. We owe it to them, don't we, to engage them in the great dialectical issues?

---

*My feelings toward the topic give me words to write. Most often I use my actual thoughts in the journal. Not the sweet coating of "good" sound stuff, but the real bitter words. Truth.*

—Heather Wade

But in the weave of prompts we must remember, too, kids' *kidness*. If each journal day they enter the classroom and behold on the board a solemn, oppressive prompt, they'll soon turn off, and the journal process will lack joy entirely, collapse under its own ponderous weight.

The process is a rhythm, and every so often we have to quicken that rhythm by introducing a light-hearted prompt, perhaps such as this:

*In a dream a voice comes to you: "My friend, when you wake up you will have the power, for one day only, to be invisible. Simply say the word 'kazaam,' and you'll be so. Say 'kazoom,' and you'll be back."*

*Strange dream, you think, but when you wake up you find it's true. You say the words, and they work!*

*What would you do that day? You have twenty-four hours to move through the world either completely invisible, invisible sometimes, or visible all the time, as we are.*

*Would you stay around your family and friends? Would you travel through the countryside or through the city? Would you play tricks, using your voice sometimes?*

*Think about it. Write about it.* (Journal Prompt #60)

Or a similarly attractive topic. Prompts like these often serve to engage kids who don't respond well to the weightier ones, enfranchising those same kids into the journal effort: the journal *community*, we might say, though that word has been used almost to death.

*Well, since I'm writing a story called the "Glass Dragon," when I'm describing the main character I try to put some attributes of mine in that person. I would write like this: Zack is a knight, but not an ordinary knight, a knight with vast power who starves for perfection.*

—Patrick Medina

## FLUENCY JOURNALS AS "SAFE HAVENS"

Indeed, though, we teachers *are* establishing a writing community when we use Fluency Journals in our classrooms. The effort, though individually realized, has a community energy to it, and you'll soon feel it. Journal Day takes on a life of its own—not simply of comfortable routine, though some comfort there exists—but of shelter: a dignified place a student can enter without fear either of interruption or of judgment.

Lately, I'm learning more deeply about the function of the Fluency Journals as a shelter for students. Whether students are upper-middle-class or extremely poor, they have precious little privacy in their lives, and the idea of "safe haven" for them is rare, if it exists at all. The upper-middle-class girl may get a ride to school with a parent, meet friends at the gate, go to her intensely busy classes, be whisked off after school to ballet lessons, come home, shovel in a quickly made dinner, do her homework, and go to bed. The student from a family of lower socioeconomic level may ride the city bus, arrive at that same gate, go to the same classes, go to basketball practice, come home to two brothers and two sisters, do homework, and go to bed in a room that sleeps five.

The upshot? No privacy, no time to think, to explore thoughts and beliefs. (Even at school, desks are often not desks at all but tables, commonly shared among four or five students.)

Fluency Journals, then, provide an often-revered private, pensive space in which students can explore not only their own lives but the issues, large and small, that confront them.

*Sometimes I dream of what I'm going to write about. It just kind of comes to me and then I think of what details I could add and, could it interest people who will read it?*

—Konstantin Solodukhin

## CHOOSING A PROMPT

We teachers know our classes: their abilities, their moods, and the individual "chemistry" of each class. We know what literature or history we're working on, and what the events of the day are: news stories local, national, and international, and what issues have arisen in school lately. And we know what went on in class *yesterday*.

*One thing I write about is September 11th. I get to get out all that anger I have inside.*

—Rosa Palacios

Similarly, as creative beings we want to follow our whims or hunches sometimes, too, and following those hunches when it comes to appropriate topics of the day can pay great dividends.

So the prompts in this book are not offered as occurring in any particular order, nor do they march in a specified direction. Kids would soon lose patience with prompts that remained on the lighter side (that new board game they invent, that day they're invisible), and they would sour quickly if every prompt offered were heavy-handed (the nature of death or the prevalence of child abuse).

Vary the prompts, then, and tap into topical issues that come up from day to day. Humorous or serious, day-to-day events that occur can be hot: the energy's already there, and you, as teacher, need simply adapt a prompt—or devise a new one—to get kids writing.

In my classes, as discussed in Chapter Three, I usually begin with the "journal on journals," then, next time, go to a rather serious prompt that shows kids I take them seriously. Beyond that, the decision is a day-to-day one, sometimes based on issues that came up in class the day before, other times reflecting my own preoccupations or mood or whim, and still other times reflecting my role as the conductor who makes sure that the journals themselves change moods when the energy needs a boost or when the energy needs taming.

This book supplies you with 150 prompts, of varying degrees of intensity, and on widely and wildly differing subjects.

However, day-to-day issues arise, and you may indeed want to develop your own prompts. How you'll ultimately decide to do it will reflect who you are, your voice and perspective, but I'll lay out the process of how I develop prompts, and you may want to start your own prompt-writing adventure with that framework in mind. (If you haven't already, it might be a good idea to flip forward to Part Four, the selection of prompts toward the end of the book, before proceeding; you'll get a sense of topics, length, and rhythm.)

Fundamental to the process of writing prompts is what's already been discussed in this book: that too often kids are given terse, thin prompts that are both extremely ambiguous and "clueless." One can certainly make the case that a gifted writer can take something as diminutive as a phrase and go with it: turn out an accomplished piece of writing—creative or expository—based on the germ of the idea contained within that phrase.

Sure. But most kids are not (yet) gifted writers, and they need help: not a crutch but a ladder upward. The speaker in Robert Frost's subtly skillful "After Apple-Picking" recalls the actual feel of the rounded rung of his orchard ladder. We want kids rhetorically to know that ladder, recall the feel of it underfoot in their ascent toward the harvest of effective writing.

So if I'm asking kids to write in a well-developed way, I need to offer in return a well-developed prompt. Here are the topic *bodies* that I tend to go after:

- Topics I know kids are interested in
- Topics I'm interested in, and suspect that kids might be interested in, too, even if they involve the deep life struggles—philosophical, emotional, ethical, even physical
- Topical issues precipitated by the news: not sensationalist detritus, but issues offering universal questions or ramifications

- Really silly ideas that enter my mind: the what-ifs we sometimes consider
- Issues arising from conversation with students in class, in the hall, school news, or particular characters' dilemmas in the literature or history that we might be reading

## CRAFTING PROMPTS OF YOUR OWN

As described, these prompts can sound quite straitlaced. They're not. In the section containing prompts, the overall categories cover a wide-ranging palette, from "Goofy and Imaginative" to "Deep Life Issues." The main point is to get the kids past the simple exposition of events ("I woke up at 7:00 this morning.").

Now: What to do when you as a teacher have the germ of a topic and want to write a useful prompt? There are a couple of ways to approach it. Here's one way:

1. Start with an introductory background sentence:

   *There are lots of things in life that we wish didn't happen. Some things we have control of, but many things are completely out of our control.*

2. Then, move on to an essential question:

   *What is one thing you wish didn't happen?*

3. Then, offer some suggestions, from the larger world:

   *Perhaps that thing was a world-affecting event: global warming, or the atomic bombs on Hiroshima and Nagasaki, for example.*

4. Then, spiral inward, toward self:

   *Or perhaps that thing was our own "personal" atomic bomb: something that happened in our lives that we wish we could erase.*

5. Show understanding of the myriad possibilities:

   *Maybe we had control over the way it went, or maybe we just observed, completely impotent (without power).*

6. Now get the writing going:

   *Write about it, and, if you can, write about how we—or you—can "move on" with life, using that event as a* lesson *from which to learn.*

That's one way. Another way goes like this:

1. Begin with a question:

   *Is there a* photograph *that you or your family members have taken that means a lot to you?*

2. Then, again, open up the possibilities:

   *Maybe the photograph is of terrific quality—an enlarged family portrait—or maybe it's of relatively poor quality—a small, badly focused snapshot taken at a birthday party, for example. It's not the* quality *of the picture we're talking about here; it's the* content.

3. Now, ask some questions: questions from which kids can build paragraphs.

   *What is it in that photograph that means something to you? Are there people in it who are (were?) important to you? Are there details in it—things in the background, an expression on someone's face, perhaps, that "move you" emotionally, or trigger further memories?*

4. And again, get the writing going:

   *Write about that photograph. Be as detailed as possible, and be sure to talk about* why *it's important to you.*

*—A few quick notions. One is that when I use a word the kids might not know, I'll often put a simple translation next to it in parentheses. Another is that prose written on the board for adolescents seems to work best when it's occasionally laced with little utterances ("Yecch!"), goofy questions within parentheses ("Are you one of those people who look as if they don't worry, but really do?"), and—much to the chagrin of teachers of dignified diction—copious underlines and exclamation marks. These things do heighten the interest level.*

You can see, then, reader, that the essential tone of each prompt, one hopes, is that of acceptance: that there are no wrong responses, and that we as teachers recognize each human life as embodying different experiences and perspectives. Further, each prompt holds not only its essential question (theme) but questions within that larger question, each of which can result in a paragraph. (Certainly, those skilled writers we've discussed won't need such "station markers"; they'll prefer their own *tour de force*. And certainly, these questions-within-questions do not always, if taken sequentially by tentative writers, make for the most smoothly transitioned prose. But the writing gets down on paper, the basic expectation of volume is understood, and the structure itself is growing foundationally.)

So: a question or a background statement to begin. Then an exegesis of different ways of feeling and thinking about the issue ("Some people say . . . but other people contend," or the like), an opening up of thinking possibilities, questions, more questions, and finally an exhortation to write. It's fairly simple, and as you review the prompts in this book, you'll quickly pick up the pattern and easily be able to make your own.

# Working with the Prompts in the Classroom

**W**rite the prompt on the board: the whole prompt, either verbatim from this book or adapted to your needs. (But if you do adapt it, try not to cut it much: its impact is commensurately diminished, and the *raison d'être* for the prompt's structure disappears.) If your handwriting is horrible, print. The whole effort's a little laborious; it takes five minutes or so, and you have to budget for that. *But it's worth every calorie burned, every minor ache of your writing arm.*

Over the years I had an inkling that my physical writing of the prompts on the chalkboard made a difference, though I wasn't sure. The act of writing—that board seeming to burst its seams with words—certainly conveyed seriousness on my part, but so what?

Last year the kids gave me the *so what.* Meredith and I did a little end-of-year evaluation of the journal process, asking kids both to write and to speak about how the journal process works for them. She asked one class, "What if the journal prompts weren't written on the board, but, instead, on journal day, you got a piece of paper with the prompt printed at the top?"

The students reacted with revulsion: hoots and boos, the idea shot down furiously.

"Why not?" I asked. "I could simply type them up on the computer and photocopy them. And after all, you guys always complain that my handwriting is so horrible!"

"It wouldn't be the same," said the kids. "It would be like just any assignment we get all day, and this is special."

And they're right. The handwritten prompts *are* special: they're written just for them. (True, if you have multiple classes, it's for those others too, but we don't have to proclaim *that* from the town hall tower, do we?) That sense of "specialness"—personalness—seems to be an essential ingredient in the fuel for both process and product.

## REINFORCING THE PROMPTS BEFORE THE WRITING BEGINS

It doesn't work simply to say, *OK, everyone: read the prompt on the board and write on that, please.* No: the laying down of the prompt needs to be clear, predictable, and reinforced.

As noted with the journal protocol script, I'll usually start out by saying,

> *Would anyone like to read today's prompt out loud?*

The prompts are usually interesting enough to elicit a few raised hands: students willing to take a chance.

> *Great* [I'll say for the first time or two], *if you can read my writing, Robert, give it a try!*

Robert *will* give it a try, often successfully. You help him along with words he can't decipher or with vocabulary he might not know. Your job is to keep the energy going, the sense intact, the interest high. Then you paraphrase, reiterating and explicating the prompt a quick second time around to catch the kids who may have drifted as Robert was reading.

> *Terrific, Robert. Thanks. So: as you can see, today's prompt is about happiness and joy. I'm asking whether you think there are differences between happiness and joy, and what those differences might be. Some people think they're just the same, and some kids, in the past, have*

*—It's important to do that quick oral recap at the end of the student reading. You'll see that it really pulls many kids in, serves to synthesize.*

> *—The effectiveness of this oft-repeated phrase was brought home to me recently when, in the context of their working silently on a test, I said to the kids, "Quiet time." A student reflexively, almost unconsciously, said, "Quiet time, Journal Time."*

> *written that they're really different. And remember as you're writing that examples are really interesting to read and smart to use.*
>      *Are there any questions? No? OK, everybody. Quiet time, Journal Time.*

Every time, that's repeated: Quiet time, Journal Time.

Now you hit the "Play" button on the CD.

## ADDRESSING STUDENT QUESTIONS

Sometimes, after your introduction to the prompt, kids will ask questions. If the questions are relevant to understanding the nature of the prompt, answer them out loud, briefly. If they're tangential, clearly far from any relation to the prompt, respond quickly and gently: tell the student you'll come and talk about it during  Journal Time. And if they're more in the nature of commentary—oral response to the prompt on the board, respond briefly in kind, then simply say:

> *All right, guys: this is fun to talk about, but let's remember that this is about writing: let's write about it.*

Truncate further conversation immediately, and continue:

> *Let's get to work.*

It's easy to get drawn into discussion about the topic, but more than a few seconds of oral discussion tends ultimately, for some reason I haven't yet understood, to diminish both the amount and variety of writing on the prompt.

## STUDENTS' OWN PROMPTS

At a certain point early in the year, students may ask if they themselves can write out a prompt on the board as the day's topic.

The answer is *yes*, but that answer, based again on my experience of early error, defers the issue for a while:

> *Yes—sure, I'll let you guys come up with your own topics. Not right away, though. Soon enough, and we'll be talking about that at the time. But yes, the answer is yes.*

Why defer them when the energy seems to be there now? Because the rhythm and fullness and typical diction of the prompts have not settled into them yet. The teacher who, at this early point, asks students to write prompts, receives in return thin and underdeveloped core ideas that may be great, but that are difficult to write about.

"Plan B" works, and it's this. Sometime midyear, the kids come in and find there's nothing on the board on a journal day. You say,

> *OK, you guys, do you remember when early in the year you asked if you could write prompts of your own? Well, I think the time has come. Think about the structure of the prompts I put on the board. I usually start with a statement or a question, right? Then I go into detail about that statement or question, asking more questions inside of questions. Have you noticed that? Good.*
>
> *And how many of you have found it easy to write in that format?* [Lots of hands are raised.] *Good. So: today during Journal Time you'll be writing journal prompts that you think kids would like to write on. I'd like you to write three prompts during today's journal session. Think about things teachers might never ask kids to write about—keep it clean, my friends: I have to read these!—and write good, strong prompts based on your ideas.*

This, of course, is an optional activity: a student who wants to write on another topic certainly may. And while the kids are writing—and many will choose to invent prompts today—pull out that old cardboard shoe box you've been saving for some such reason, cover it in colored paper, cut a little "mail slot" in the top, write "Journal Prompts" on it in big, bold letters, and put it at the side of the room. Then, when writing time is finished, pass out scissors, have kids cut their prompts into strips, pass around the shoe box, and have kids stuff them in.

*Do we have to put our names on these?*

*No: but if you want to, you may.*

Then, later in the day, sift through them and toss out the obscene or silly scatological ones: there will be a few, but the bulk will be in earnest, and what you'll find will be surprisingly well-developed, interesting prompts.

What's happened? Kids have internalized the thinking and writing template that you've written on the board for months now, and such manifestation in these student-written prompts is a measure of victory on your part. Think of it: a multilayered, focused template able to be put into place—the topic with its loyal implicit questions in attendance—at any moment. You can surmise that if they're able to *generate* good prompts, they're able to use that same template to generate fully fleshed-out writing.

---

*You can cheat a little on journals because usually Mr. Fleming puts like a paragraph on the board, you can copy one or two sentences. You can connect something to that because it's already helping you think and continue. You can also extend your sentences and add more details. Always keep on thinking, no matter how hard it is.*

---

—Jessica Chen

*—Student journal prompts: If you use one on the board (you've cleaned up the grammar), simply write "Student Prompt" at the top of the board. That simple notation often injects an extra boost or cachet to the prompt, and lots of good writing can come from it.*

*—There will always be one student or other who says, day after day, "Do we have to write on this?" To which you'll respond: "What are our rules about writing on the prompt?" Another student will say, "It's not mandatory unless he says so!" And you respond: "And how often will the prompts be mandatory?" "Almost never!" a student will call out. "There's your answer," you say. If this pattern continues, it's good to review, before introducing journals one day, the wide options available for kids and the fact that you'll rarely require that they write on a topic.*

## CHOOSING SKILLED PROMPT READERS

As the weeks go by, certain students will continue to volunteer to read the prompts. It's *very* difficult for classmates to listen to a plodding, error-ridden reading of the prompt by a low-skilled reader, no matter how sweet and well-intentioned the student is, no matter how egalitarian the teacher. Such readings take extra time and drain energy from the prompt itself, and the journals that day get off to a languid start. Choose, then, from among five or six students who can consistently read your handwriting and read at a brisk enough pace—even if you're plugging in a word now and then—to keep the sense of the thing alive.

**PART THREE**

# Speed

## The Writing Practice

# chapter SEVEN

# Motivation and Feedback

The most difficult part is over for you: you've laid down the track. You've paid careful attention to the symbolic importance of the kids' actual folders, you've chosen a responsible kid to pass those folders out, you've given the kids a step-by-step, clear introduction to the process, you have a sense of the scope and range of the prompts, you have a predictable schedule, and the music is ready to do its work.

What to do now? Kick back and relax during the process? Ah, but we teachers know better. We know that any solid project, once begun, must be encouraged— sometimes goosed, goaded—then maintained. The maintenance is year-round, and will be discussed shortly. But the encouragement must be felt immediately.

## ENCOURAGEMENT DURING EARLY SESSIONS

The first few sessions are essential to the success of your Fluency Journals. Your own focus and attention these days will move you toward sustainable success, but your inattention will be read as lack of commitment on your part and will result in the journals' early collapse.

For the first ten minutes of these two or three sessions, you slowly circulate around the room. The prompt is on the board, has been read, and the kids have begun writing. There's a palpable sense of stress in the room, for many students are not sure they'll be able to succeed. It's a tension to be concerned about, and a tension whose energy must be put to use.

You're quiet, you don't say a word to anyone, but your body language says it all. You catch the eye of a kid who's writing madly and flash a "thumbs up." You see another kid speaking to a neighbor and you approach wordlessly and shake your

*—Lately I've been asking kids to have everything off of their desks before jour-nal begins, the journal folders the only thing in their field of vision. This gives them more room to write and diminishes distraction.*

finger back and forth at them, a gesture that, one step up from the old finger-to-the-lips, indicates your seriousness about the protocol. You briefly pat another on the back as she's intently writing. You do a little abbreviated pump of the fist as another student looks up from his concentrated, already lengthy prose.

Then, during that first one, two, or even three sessions, you do something you'll very rarely do the rest of the year. You go to the stereo, turn the music down, briefly interrupt the writ-ing, and say, in one variation or another, this truth:

*I won't be interrupting this music much, but I just have to say that I'm seeing such amazing writing going on here. Great job, everybody.*

You mean it: you *are* seeing amazing writing going on, and the phenomenon is worthy of respectful recognition. You turn up the music again.

Ten minutes of this hovering is fine, but much more than that makes the kids nervous—makes them feel as if you're some kind of official Word Police Helicopter. After ten minutes or so, I often will take out a journal I keep in the classroom and write a little in it. I don't do this all year, for reasons I'll explain later, but on these first days I do.

Where do I write? Ha—on the paper, sure, but it's the *where* in the classroom that's of importance here.

It seems to me that a teacher who wants to create an early sense of community in the Fluency Journal process ought not to sit royally at the teacher's desk, but rather sit among the kids in a student chair, alternating around the class as the year goes on. This is of course a good general idea for any teacher wanting to build community, but seems especially important in the journal process, for soon you'll be asking if any students want to share their journals by reading them aloud, and an authoritarian teacher behind a Formica-and-metal desk is hardly a presence that invites the relaxed confidence that engenders volunteerism.

So you're there, now, writing, and five minutes before the twenty minutes' end, you say, gently,

> *Five minutes left, everyone.*

Same time-warning given at two minutes, then, at the end of the twenty-minute session, you say something to this effect:

> *OK, now, everyone: put the last few words on this baby, 'cause this baby's going to bed.*

Now:

> *Maria—would you quietly collect the journals, please? Oh, wait a minute, Maria—would anyone like to read theirs?*

If you get a volunteer, you're on your way toward community. If not, don't worry. Soon they'll be asking to read, but for today you'll say,

> *That's OK. Some other time, maybe somebody will be ready to read. Go ahead and pick them up, Maria.*

—*As the year goes on and the journal process becomes deeper, you'll see kids writing in a way that is more and more engrossed. Sometimes it's a phenomenon of a particular class. Other times, it seems to be a particular topic that has struck home. Other days, there may only be some charge in the air, but it's obvious that to stop the amazing (and often very moving) writing energy would almost be a crime against nature. On those days, with about two minutes left, I'll say, "How many kids would like a few more minutes?" The hands will shoot up: 80 percent of them. "OK, let's make it five more, then." "Ten!" a few will urge. "Seven," I'll say, keeping the "carrot" fresh in this gamesmanship, the desirable thing desirable, the idea of writing as a pleasure alive, if only in kids' subconscious.*

At the end of the first session, try to say something like:

> *That session went really well. Good job, you guys. Could you hear the quiet? Great. That makes for good concentration, good writing.*
> *Now: how many kids wrote more than you thought you'd be able to write?*

Many hands will go up.

> *Terrific! You'll be shocked at how much you can write.*

Now, to solidify the kids' sense of the project's overarching meaning:

> *Just one more thing: how many kids are hoping that their writing improves this year?*

Lots of hands should go up. (God, if they don't, we're in trouble!)

> *Great. I admire you for that. Well, I'll just say this: if you take this journal process seriously this year, I can almost guarantee that your writing will improve—not only in fluency, but in what you're able to write about and in your strategies for writing. So we're off to a good start, everybody. This is fun.*

---

> *When I first became an eighth grader, I couldn't write much. I hated writing. But in this class I started to write more than usual. I can write a page and a half or so, but at home I just can't think of anything to write about. Maybe I need some music. . . . I think instead of having journals on Tuesdays and Thursdays, it should be on Mondays, Wednesdays and Fridays because that gives us three days of the week to write.*

---

—Daniel O'Meara

## THE TEACHER'S ROLE DURING JOURNAL TIME

I know that some teachers and writers believe strongly that if the kids are being asked to write, the teacher should be writing as well. As mentioned earlier, I think this is a good idea in the beginning—a teacher writing with the rest of the group does invoke a seriousness—but as the year goes on I have found it impossible, and impractical, to write with the kids consistently.

Why? For a number of reasons.

First, in most urban and dynamic suburban schools, Journal Time for the teacher is not a time to get lost in dreamy writer's thoughts: not a time to paddle along in the slowly flowing waters of prose. Your job is to keep an eye on the kids, and if your classroom is like mine, you may have as many as thirty-six. You need to make sure that all is well, take the temperature of how the day's prompt is energizing the class, and be available for students when they need you. Remember: it's quiet time, and if the kids have gotten the protocol down well enough, they'll be simply raising their hands, not calling out, during writing time. So if you're off in your own writing world, you're essentially forcing kids who have a quick question to breach one of the rules you've worked so hard to establish—*no voices*—simply in order to rouse you from your writing reverie.

So what to do? As soon as the music is put on, I go to the little whiteboard in the corner and scribble out the name of the musician playing, along with the title of the piece. Then I sit among the kids during journal session. (Yes, once in a while, I may go to the computer at the side of the room to finish printing something, but that's rare.) I'll often go to my desk, grab a stack of papers from students in *that* class, and read papers as the students write. Other times, I'll read a student's journal and make comments in the margins (see Chapter Nine on assessment), having left the student with the paper on which to write today's entry.

The point is this: be *with* the students, both psychologically and physically, during journal. If a phone call comes through during Journal Time (as phone calls will) and you have to answer it, do so in a low voice, showing both respect for writers in the room and reinforcing the room's overall tone—a tone you don't want to lose. Then quit the call as soon as possible.

Perhaps it goes without saying, but just in case it doesn't, here are a few things a teacher ought not to do during Journal Time:

- Leaving the room
- Kicking back at the teacher's desk and loudly sipping a cup of coffee
- Making a snack in the microwave
- Frantically word-processing at the computer or avidly checking e-mail
- Conversing loudly with any student, class member, or visitor
- Allowing a visitor to continue speaking loudly and brashly, oblivious to what's happening in the room
- Interrupting students—singly or collectively—to discuss other business
- Making calls on the classroom phone, within the school or outside
- Pulling kids off their journals to do errands or clerical work

Each of these will undercut your program, will demonstrate to students that you don't practice what you preach, and implicitly will give students the idea that you regard the Journal Time as busywork for them, and that they, therefore, should not take it seriously.

## REINFORCING THE ENERGY

Things are rolling along pretty well now. The kids understand the protocol and routine, they're taking comfort in the predictability of journal day (often saying, "We're doing journal today, right?" as they walk in the room); they're not snickering any more at the music but seem to be listening, heads cocked; they're curious about and engaged by the prompts, and—thanks to your vigilance—almost every student is on task during Journal Time.

How do you keep it going? How can such energy and concentration be sustained for an entire school year?

## IMMEDIATE FEEDBACK

The first way to keep the energy flowing is by giving immediate feedback. As noted, you've already "fed back" during the first few sessions very briefly by interrupting the session to admire the amount of writing going on. You've "fed back" oral comments to kids who choose to stand proudly at the podium and read their journals. Your responses have been respectful and admiring, not at all negatively critical, for you know that negative criticism on the teacher's part in a project such as this only serves to dissolve the determination of students who thought they might one day get up and read.

Now four other ways of early feedback are essential to getting the process "into the groove"—a groove as deep and solid as those chariot-tracks one encounters carved into the marble streets of Pompeii.

The first is a little public display. You say something like this:

> *I've been looking at your journals, you guys, and they're wonderful. Lots of writing, lots of care, lots of thinking. Is there anyone who'd let me just quickly hold up some papers to show what I'm talking about?*

One or two students certainly will raise hands.

> *Don't worry—nobody'll read 'em. I just want to quickly flash them around to show what great work people are doing.*

You take one of those journals, remove the sheaf of papers on which there's copious writing, and do a little public flip-through for the class to see.

> *Wow. Nice work, Angela. Lots of effort there. Can I do one more?*

You do the same for Philip's journal, same admiration.

> *And I wish we had time to show lots of these, you guys, but we'd better get going. I just wanted you to see what kids are doing—lots of kids are headed for a wonderful grade in journals.*

The second is easily reinforced by asking kids privately—during a classroom break or as they gather their books and backpacks to get to their next class—what topic they wrote on. *What'd you write on in journal today, Pete? Ah, the Giants! God, they really melted down, didn't they?*

Little exchanges like that: relaxed but real.

The third way of keeping the process energized is to ask, once every few journal sessions,

> *Just wondering: how many kids wrote on the prompt?*

Students raise hands, tentatively the first few times you ask it. Soon they see that they're not alone, that it's not nerdy to write on the teacher's topic, and they take encouragement from that. (This is also a great way of gauging the class—its interest in certain types of prompts, or "where they are" mentally.)

The fourth way to reinforce the energy, this one deeper and more long-lasting, is to give kids written feedback either immediately (that day) or in the short term (within a week or two). I try to make it a habit during the first two weeks—especially with classes that are a little recalcitrant or lower-skilled than others—to pull the journals and give kids early positive feedback. This feedback need not be fawning and disingenuous, and certainly can include some gently corrective shepherding. But early words from the teacher help give kids a sense that they're going in the right direction—or, if not, what they need to do to get moving in that direction. And early words from a teacher strengthen the students' realization that they have responsibility toward the journals: a responsibility that the teacher is serious about—and will keep track of.

You'll find a fuller discussion of feedback and evaluation in the next chapter, but for now, on these early comments, let's just focus on what seems to work. Let's assume that the kids have written four journal entries so far, and you review the journals. Here's what seems most effective toward galvanizing energy at this point:

- Quick comments in the margins: "I'm enjoying reading this!"; "You're off to a good start, Phil!"; "The Giants really blew it this year, didn't they!"

- A summary comment, written on the student's paper, just after the most recent journal entry: "Phil, you're off to a good start. Bravo! Lots of writing here! (Remember paragraphing, Phil.)" Or: "Mei Lin, I've enjoyed reading what you've got so far. It seems that you're *liking* the topics so far. Next time, try to respond to *all* the questions inside the prompt, OK, and I bet you'll write a lot more!" And so on. (This certainly is the appropriate place to urge kids to follow the protocol on margins, relative neatness, and so on. It wouldn't be fair to them if you didn't mention it now, in this early read, and then lowered their grade because of it later. Be honest with them now, and they'll respect that.

- The day after your quick reviews of the journals, another pep talk is indicated. It needn't be long:

*I just wanted to mention that I quickly read your journals last night, you guys. Lots of impressive work in there. Very impressive. A few kids need to remember our rules for margins, a few other kids need to remember to put titles on, a few others need to remember to date their papers, and let's see: what else. Oh! Paragraphs! Please remember about changing paragraphs, everybody!*

*But overall, terrific. You guys are going to be shocked at how your writing will expand this year. Good job. You'll see a few of my comments in your journals.*

You can see that the "carrot" approach works better in the Fluency Journal process than the stick.

(Is there any "stick" at all? Is it never necessary? Well, yes, on occasion, though the stick itself is shaped like a carrot. More about that in Chapter Nine.)

## THE POWER OF VOLUNTEER READERS

You may decide not to do this, for it does take time, but I find that on particular days of high-interest topics, many kids want to read their entries aloud.

Terrific! Allowing them to read orally (I ask them to go to the lectern) not only covers a few of our oral-language subject-matter standards, it also serves many functions:

- Students reading their journals orally *model* what can be written.
- Students reading their journals orally create *community,* often through humor or pathos (OK—sometimes bathos) in the class.
- Students reading their journals orally give the *teacher* prime teaching opportunities.

## HOW TO LISTEN AND WHAT TO SAY

Let's say "Vanessa" gets up to read her journal. How do you respond? *Do* you respond?

The first notion is that teachers *listen,* and listen intently, allowing no interruptions. Many times I will choose to interrupt a student reading to say, "Excuse me, Vanessa. I'm sorry to stop you and ask you to start again, but Dante and Beatrice are talking back there, and making it impossible for the class to concentrate. Can you guys focus, please? Vanessa's reading, and she needs your attention. Begin again, please, Vanessa."

What you're doing here is *establishing a civil environment for the forum.* You're insisting that each student reader be respected, and in doing so you're also implicitly encouraging other students to be brave enough to stand behind the podium and read their own entries. They know you'll protect them.

Further, your demeanor during the reading is intent. If you miss something, stop the student, and say, "Excuse me, Vanessa: I missed that last sentence. Can you go back and repeat it? Thanks." Vanessa—and by extension the rest of the class—knows that you're really listening, and taking her writing seriously.

After Vanessa's reading, she'll most likely want to speed back to her seat.

*Wait a minute, Vanessa,* you'll say. *Stay up there for a minute. Does anyone have any quick comments on Vanessa's entry?*

It's obvious here that the teacher is seeking *positive* comments only, having established such a tone for the classroom. Someone might say, "I loved what you said about boys—they *are* mean!" And the class will have a good laugh. Someone else might say, simply, "Good writing!" and another might ask, "What Chinese restaurant were you talking about there?" Numerous comments, some about the process of writing, some not. The teacher's place in this forum? Facilitator: mover-along of the energy, keeper-of-the-positive-tone, guardian-of-time.

At the end, it's good for you to say something, too. Did Vanessa use a smart descriptive phrase? Was her dialogue realistic? Did she structure an argument well, or destroy a lurking counterargument successfully? Was there a sense of *passion* and *voice* throughout the whole thing? Great. Say it. Were there a few places that were confusing? Ask about them with interest—say that they were a little confusing, then show your new understanding when she explains them out loud. Do you want to ask if Vanessa used certain conventions, such as quotation marks, or even, at a lower level, question marks? Ask it, gently, maybe with a *just curious* overture.

Effusive praise, though, in the public forum, can sometimes be dangerous. The great and kind American poet William Stafford was famous in his college writing workshops for *not* lavishing praise, even on the best writers. Why? Well, when we think about it, and imagine ourselves as students in class that day, and we hear the teacher gushing over Vanessa's work, it's easy to imagine that the effect can be counterproductive. "God, I'll never be that good." Or "He didn't say all those things about *me* when I got up last week!"

So in hearing student work orally, I *never* say, *Gee, Vanessa, you're* such *a great writer.* I'll often say, *Terrific reading, Vanessa,* and specifically mention images or successes *within the text,* but effusiveness here can do more damage than good, and what I find is that the "reading bug" can stay contagious without a teacher's gushing.

Then, a recognition of the brave act of standing before the class: *Thanks for reading, Vanessa,* and quick teacher-led applause.

Certainly, you'll see some classes whose writers don't often want to read their work aloud. It's strange: the pattern is set relatively early in the process. In some classes a dozen hands shoot up when the *Who'd like to read his or her journal today?* question is asked. Other classes, often more circumspect but certainly quite *on task,* have few, if any, volunteers. Some classes are simply more private.

Finally, a quick mention that I don't ask for volunteer readers each day we write in our Fluency Journals. English is such a huge subject that we can't afford the time. (But if I go too many days without offering students the opportunity to read, the complaints will fly.)

Here are a few fairly typical teacher comments:

> *Aha! Stop, Vanessa, for just a minute. Sorry to interrupt, but just go back and read that first sentence again. Notice how Vanessa began with a strong statement: "I think the death penalty is ridiculous and that people who believe in it have weak brains." Such a brave first sentence! Now let's listen while she backs that bold statement up.*

Or:

> *Did anyone notice any particular details Vanessa put into her writing that made it so interesting? Right: that image of the man in the electric chair, the look in his eyes. And that image of the executioner's cold hands. Wow. Those things really bring writing alive.*

Or:

> *Vanessa—in that passage where you and your brother were having an argument—did you remember to put quotation marks around what each person said? You did? Great! And did you break a new paragraph every time a different person was speaking? Great.*

Or:

> *Vanessa, you read so quickly and covered so many ideas. It was hard for me to hear where the pauses were. Did you remember to put some paragraph breaks in there? Oops! You forgot? Oh, well—remember next time, OK?*

And then you launch into a quick, ad hoc lesson for the whole class on paragraph breaks.

I consider these moments to be among the best of teaching, really: high interest, quick lessons, teachable moments, single skills zinged home.

---

*I have also noticed that*
*my slang in writing has stopped.*

---

—Curran Wong

—*Once in a while it's a good idea to have oral readers show, visually, what their paper looks like. The papers are usually impressive, and, again, good models.*

—*Two little caveats about student oral reading after journal. If you have a chatty class or a class of extroverted high-participants, an entire class period can slip by quickly if you call on every student who wants to read. I try to limit the readings to one or two, promising other hand-raisers that they'll come next. A second alarum is that once in a while a student will stand up and read something so moving or wild or wonderful that as a teacher you're derelict if you don't defer the planned curriculum for a few minutes and discuss the nature of what that student wrote. As I write this tonight, I remember Leonette, who on the second day of journal got up and read a moment-by-moment description of the day she witnessed her father being shot and killed in Jamaica.*

*That was a day to stop and talk for a while, turning our pedagogue's eyes away from standards and high-stakes tests and toward the human children in the class.*

# Addressing Problems During Journal Time

In early years, I encountered almost every problem imaginable during Journal Time. Here are the most consistently occurring ones, and how best to deal with them.

## DISTURBANCES

It's actually fairly rare for a student to set out to disrupt Journal Time, but nonetheless, disruptions happen.

• Sometimes a student will interrupt the Journal Time with a loudly vocalized question. Wherever you are at the time, hold up your hand in the "stop" signal, put your finger to your lips in an unvocalized "shh!" and immediately walk over there. Lean down at the student's desk, and whisper something like, "Wilbur, please remember that we don't talk out loud during Journal Time. Always raise your hand quietly if you need help. Now—what did you want to ask?" Wilbur will almost always respond in kind, whispering his question. I really try to avoid *ever* vocalizing fully during Journal Time—it's too distracting for the writers, and seems hypocritical. If a consistently truculent student persists, I'll make a fairly big (quiet) deal of it, motion for him to come with me out into the hall, and firmly but briefly remind him of our *Journal Time is quiet time* mandate.

• Sometimes a student will lean over and have a whispered conversation with another student. I make sure I'm aware that this is occurring, and if I see that it goes much past a quick exchange (for goodness sake, they may be saying, "Cool topic!" or "Ever heard this kind of crazy music?"), I'll do one of a few things in the repertoire. The first is to send a "teacher stare" toward the students. That usually does the trick. The next level up is to walk over to the student's desk "on my way" somewhere (the spectacle of this is diminished and noticed less by the class if the teacher seems to be going about normal business) and, passing the talkative student's desk, knock on it twice as if I'm knocking on a door. Something kinetic about that action seems to make it work, and the student gets back on task. The third level, of course, is to lean over and talk to the student directly, repeating that mantra that *Journal Time is quiet time.*

- Once in a while you'll have a student ask you if they'll receive fewer points if they write on topics of their own. If that question is public, great: you can handle it and reinforce the idea that almost all topics are valid topics, respected equally. However, if the question is in private, it's probably a signal, again, to reinforce the *student choice* protocol with the larger class. The best time to do that is usually after the prompt-reading of the next journal day.

Often during Journal Time you'll see a kid looking up from the paper, not writing but staring. Most of the time they're simply thinking, and certainly we need time to think while we're writing! (I really enjoy some of the pensive looks kids get when they're writing these thoughtful testaments to their lives.) However, sometimes the staring seems to go on a bit long. I'll often get the student's attention from across the room by waving my hand, and simply make a silent "writing" motion, using my palm as the gestural "paper." That often works.

Paper wadders: Especially early in the process, for some low-functioning students, the frustration level can be high, and, occasionally, kids who need to call attention to themselves do so. This is usually manifest in dramatic and loud paper wadding: a few minutes pass, "John" wads a paper loudly, begins a new sheet, works for two minutes, wads again, aggressively. A teacher wants to diminish such frustration and "nip it in the bud"—it can be disruptive. (The paper wadder, for some reason, is usually a boy.) So it's important that you respond quickly. Simply walk over and say, "John, please remember that this is quiet time. Don't make those big noises with paper. It distracts students, and it bothers *me*. If you want to throw away the paper you're working on, put it aside and throw it away at the end of the period. Got it?"

*Then* it's important to work with John a little. Is he frustrated that many of the other kids seem to be writing and he's not producing much? Discreetly open the paper he's just wadded. Point out to him that there are *words* on that paper, words that *count*, and that he's discarding them.

"I didn't like what I wrote," John will say. That's your cue to remind him that you're not stressing grammatical correctness or spelling—you just want him to get his thoughts down.

"But it's not good!" John might say.

"Who says it's not good?" you reply. "I might have read it and thought it was *really* good, and your wadding it up makes it impossible for me ever to see. Right?"

John will grudgingly admit that you're right.

Now you've got him, and he's open to Frozen Writers Counseling.

---

*The trick that is really useful is that when you're writing, concentrate. Just think a lot about what you are trying to write and concentrate a lot and you will be successful. The more you concentrate, the faster you will write. That's how I do it. The more I am thinking about what I am writing is the fastest way for me.*

---

—Edgar Hernandez

## FROZEN WRITERS COUNSELING

Certainly, in almost every class, there will be students who simply aren't producing. If this occurs only once in a while in individual students, that's fairly normal: we all have tough days. But if the difficulty in writing goes on journal day after journal day, the student's self-worth as a writer is compromised, and frustration increases.

What to do?

Let's continue with "John" the paper-wadder. Here's the scenario: Journal Time is going strong for five minutes or so, the music is on. It's quiet, you're keyed in to what each student is doing, and you notice that John has either started paper-wadding or wears a sullen, frustrated look on his face.

So you grab one of the plastic chairs in your room (I liked better my little wooden stool before it disappeared), and without making a commotion, you go sit beside him. You speak quietly. You ask John what he wants to write about, and he says, "I just can't think of anything."

There are two ways to go here: the first is that you ask him whether he wants to write about the prompt on the board. "I don't know," he'll say, and there you've got your entrée: he hasn't said no.

Say the topic is the death penalty. The dialogue goes something like this:

*Do you think the death penalty is a good thing, John?*

"Uh. I'm not sure."

*Well, let's think about it. A man murders someone in a horrible way. That's the crime. Now, some people say. "An eye for an eye and a tooth for a tooth," and that he should die, because he killed a person, and no longer has the right to live."*

"Uh-huh," John says. (He's opening now—a good sign!)

*But there are other people who think that it's crazy for the state to say, "In this state you can't kill anybody. If you kill someone, we'll kill you." You know what a hypocrite is? OK. Some people say that's hypocritical. So, of the two sides—the guys who want to kill people for killing people, and the guys who think that any killing is wrong, which one do you feel closest to?*

"Uh, the other guys, I guess."

*The other guys? Which other guys?*

"The guys that say it's wrong."

*OK, so now you've got a place to start. Look up at the board now. It's asking you what you think about the death penalty—whether you believe in it or not. Now you've made a decision to write about it. You can start out by saying, simply,* I think the death penalty is wrong. *Write that now.*

John writes the sentence you've dictated.

*Now—look at the board again. Do you see the question that follows the first question? It asks you why you think it's right or why you think it's wrong. So maybe try this. Try to think of why* you *think it's wrong, and think of some crimes that you've heard of and some criminals you've heard of and use them as examples. If you just answer the questions up there one by one, and use a couple of examples, you've got a lot of writing already! OK?*

Most often John will get going. Sometimes he'll "take off," inspired, but other times he'll plod along and finish about two paragraphs or so.

Have you succeeded? I'd argue that you have. You've helped him lift himself out of temporary self-loathing, yet you haven't done his work for him (to have done so would have humiliated him), and you've given him tools to handle the *next* prompt.

Clearly, encouragement is key in John's case. It takes very little effort on the teacher's part to keep an eye on him, pass his desk at the end of the journal, and quietly say something like, *Hey, buddy—you got two good paragraphs, and by the time we finished talking, you only had ten minutes left! Not bad!*

Then there's Juan, who might also be having a hard time getting his journal off of the ground, but for different reasons.

*Are you interested in the topic today?*

"Not really."

*Do you have something in mind you want to write about?*

"Yeah, maybe my football game last Sunday. But I don't know what to say. I don't know how to start."

This is the easy one: Juan knows what he wants to write, and you simply go sequentially, and take him through the game. If you know him well, you'll know whether you need to help him by taking a few notes on a piece of scratch paper. He may not be the type: he may simply absorb what you're suggesting, step-by-step, and commit to his paper the game in its sequential steps.

But maybe not. Juan may be quite frozen, and so you help. You're his loyal note-taker.

*Who were the opponents?*

"The Spartan Boys' Club," Juan says. You write it down. You go to the next line.

*How was your team feeling before the game?*

"Really nervous—one guy threw up." You write: *Guys nervous: one guy threw up.*

*What did the coach say in the locker room before you ran onto the field?*

"He swore at us. He said we were flabby bums." Again, your pen, new line: *Coach: %&@##! Flabby bums!*

And so it goes, as Vonnegut says. A simple fleshing out of the prompt, helped along by the teacher, and in about five minutes Juan's got a writing skeleton to which he can add muscle and skin.

*OK. So—see these notes? Write a few sentences about each one, and when you get to the next one, change paragraphs. Pretty soon you'll have a lot of writing!* And you pat him once on the shoulder, grab your chair, and walk away.

True: these mediations are awfully scripted, but they work, and they're temporary. In most cases, exposed both to these mediations and orally read student models, kids soon launch out on their own.

Finally, the desperate cases. These are the kids who, on a given day, respond to none of your coaxing and cajoling. They're simply frozen, they resist the prompt on the board, and they have nothing to offer on their own. These students are difficult because it's likely they're inarticulate, and they don't drop clues, those entrées that let you follow the intricate map of your teacher-instincts. There's no "topography" to follow here. These are the "I dunno" kids, and my response to them, early in the year, goes something like this.

*OK, Sean. It sounds as if you're not interested in the topic today, right?*
"Uh."

*And you don't have anything else in mind that you might like to write about, that I can help you with?*
"Uh."

*Well, what'd you do last weekend?*
"Nothin'."

*OK. Nothing much on the weekend, eh? All right, then: you've just become a detective who was standing right by your side all day Sunday. Did you go out on Sunday?*
"Nope."

*So you didn't go out on Sunday. Great. The detective stays home with you. All day. What time did you wake up?*
"Nine."

*All right. Nine.* And you write on a sheet of Sean's paper: *I woke up at nine.*

Then you take Sean, moment by moment, through the first hour of his life on Sunday, one paragraph, written in your hand. Deadly boring prose, certainly, but it's *material,* and if you stay with him for just a little while, you'll find something that sparks an interest: even if it's only *yours,* for such a spark will raise the emotional level a bit.

*Now it's your turn, Sean. Take it hour by hour. You can do it.* The upshot: Sean writes, for that day, what you've cautioned other students *against:* a mere recapitulation of one day in his life. You've broken protocol, but it's worth it. Remember that the other kids are writing away, that the music is on, and that your conversation is private. Furthermore, no one but you and Sean will see the contents of his journal. And at the end of Journal Time you can approach Sean's desk, as another day in another situation you passed by John's, uttering a little encouragement: *Hey, Sean—you got a lot of writing out of that Sunday, eh? Next time try to attack the topic, and I'll help you if you want.*

What do these small interventions do?

What's primary is that they are not confrontational: no *"You will write in your journal, and you will do it now!"* None of that: such behavior is anger-based, spreads

*—One teacher has reported success in having her nonstarters begin by writing the prompt itself. Where generally I might say that this exercise is a time-waster, perhaps something can be said for the idea that kinetically some kids are able to get it a little better if it's written by and in their own hand; and perhaps a further case can be made for the idea that the fact that they are writing, have something on the page before beginning their response, and then the flow can begin for them. (Would you need to adjust your evaluative response for kids who write the prompt? Probably, but the problem certainly isn't an intractable one.)*

fear, and decimates the "we're-in-this-together-toward-the-great-goal-of-skilled-writing" feeling that you've worked so hard to build.

You have approached, you have sat beside them, John and Juan and Sean, as their *partner*—as someone who wants to help them succeed, who has a few tricks up his sleeve to get the flow going, and who expresses confidence in *each* of them: a confidence that *next time* they'll be on their own and independent.

Again, these little investments, still early in the year, pay off. The prose you read from John or Juan or Sean may not be Faulkner, may more resemble an enfeebled Hemingway, but it's *writing*, and it's likely that none of them has ever written so much before.

# Assessment, Response, and Grading

We've spoken of the importance of giving kids early feedback during the initial weeks of their journal experience, and of how this attentive response on the teacher's part bolsters the journals' importance.

Now for the big stuff: the weightier read, word-for-word at high speed. You'll do this for the first grading period or two, then, if you're like me, you will slightly alter the routine later in the year.

In thinking about *approach,* there are a few ways to go.

The first method surely is best, and serves well the disciplined teacher whose private life is fairly predictable, and who's not too involved with beyond-school activities. This way also suits a teacher committed to staying after school an hour or two a day, and whose classroom after school is a quiet space conducive to uninterrupted concentration. These teachers are enviable to me: they're highly organized and can find the time to read student journals a few a day, after school on site or at home.

Then there's the other group, of which I (sheepishly) admit membership: those whose lives are fairly frantic, whose classrooms after school tend to be noisy and social, and who find it difficult to carve out an hour or two—either at school or at home—to read journals. Perhaps our classrooms are used for another program after school. Perhaps it's impossible to get uninterrupted quiet in our sociable schools. Perhaps we have our own kids, and our family life exerts its formidable demands. For whatever reason, I find myself taking big rubber-banded stacks of journals home one weekend before the grading period ends and reading them on that weekend.

I hope that nowhere in this book have I represented this project as being *easy* on the teacher. It is true that if the regimen described herein is followed, the teacher has, twice a week for twenty minutes at a time, an in-class "off-stage" presence: very valuable in providing a sense of calm "breathing space" during the frantic school day. But it is also true that *reading* the journals, if that reading is done honestly, is an impressive endeavor, and one that takes a great amount of time.

My family at home is quite familiar with the stack of yellow or red or manila folders on the dining room table, and my extended family is equally familiar with my trudging into a vacation house we've rented, my suitcase on one arm, journals under the other. It's part of a teacher's life, in one manifestation or another: we know it.

All of this is a way of saying, as the Robert Frost poem exhorts, *provide, provide.* Provide time for yourself, during at least one weekend per grading period, to read and respond to journals.

Exactly how much time is necessary? That depends on your class sizes and upon how many of your classes are engaged in the journal process. Are you lucky enough to have only fifteen kids or so? Your reading task is fairly easy: a few hours for a grading period's worth of journals. Are your classes like so many others in our perennially underfunded public schools, accommodating (badly) as many as forty students? Your reading task is appreciably more, and, if you stop for breaks and pace yourself, you'll get your grading period's journals finished during one weekend. It's big, and any suggestion that it's not is delusional.

Is it worth the effort, the time subtracted from your private life?

I think so. What I learn *about* my students—their lives, their passionate opinions, their strengths and weaknesses in reading and writing, their yearnings, their burning desire to learn—makes the entire reading marathon well worth it to me. God knows that at the end of each school year, all teachers feel either twinges or paroxysms of guilt that they didn't get to know their students well enough. And at this point in my career I can't imagine what it would be like on that last June day if I hadn't read these magnificent journals: not only for their transcendent beauty, but also because it keeps me close not only to individual kids but to the lodestone: the reality in kids' lives that we teachers so easily forget.

I get a sense of kids' heroism—the enormous adversity some face, either in poverty or in emotional aridity. I learn things I didn't know: that Michelle's mother died last year (she'd never mentioned it—why should she?); that Lizzie is passionately involved every weekend in ballroom dancing, and hopes for a new partner who can tango better than the last; that Peter loves mysteries—and has devoted every page of his journal to a real *noir* gumshoe serial; that I'd (unintentionally) embarrassed Carita one day and her loyal friend Lisa has taken me to task for it, skewering me righteously (and rightfully). I learn *so* much.

Certainly I don't delude myself: not all students are forthcoming in their journals, and the simple act of reading Fluency Journals—no matter how deep the subject—does not immediately confer either broad or deep knowledge of individual students' hopes, dreams, and private lives. But it's immensely better than the alternative: a series of scattershot writing assignments of no depth whatever, perfunctorily read by a profoundly bored teacher.

So I do it, and assert further here that I emerge bleary-eyed from the entire process with a much-sharpened sense of my students' skill levels—an unambiguous knowledge from which I can teach.

(And, as mentioned before, it is possible to diminish the gross number of reading hours as the year goes on. More on that later.)

## HOW TO READ THE JOURNALS

Just before you collect the journals for your home reading, have kids put their journals in order by date. Then, pass around a stapler and have them staple that grading period's dated journals in the left-hand corner, the least recent on top, the most recent on bottom. Next, circulate a single wide-nibbed felt-tip pen of a dark color (let's say blue), and have each student mark a quick blue "slash" on the top page of their stapled journals. (The reason? Now you'll know that the first grading period's work is the "blue" sheaf, and *next* grading period you won't waste time wading into them again. Next grading period you'll have the kids "tick" their journals with a red marker, and so on, through the year.) Each new grading period's unread work is placed by students *on top* of the others, so that you don't have to dig for it.

You arrive home with an armload of journals, and when the time is right, begin reading.

If students have followed your protocol (and first grading period, there will be some who didn't), each journal entry will have a title that acts as a quick key to propel you into what they're writing about.

Here's how I handle reading the journals:

I go quickly, often passing my hand over the paper in the old speed-reading way. I *do* read, or try to read (sometimes the handwriting is horrible, and this is an issue that must be addressed immediately with that student), every word. It seems strange to say, but after all these years of reading thousands of pages of journals, I'm still interested. This is not to say that everything that every student says is interesting—only that I never come away from any journal-reading session without having read something remarkable, either in its content or in its expression.

## COMMENTING ON THE WRITTEN ENTRIES

Meredith has created a taxonomy of teacher responses to the Fluency Journals (sometimes it's difficult for the practitioner objectively to see his own practice) for your reference in Appendix C. I'll relate here what I *try* to do.

I try to give students a sense that I have read the words they've worked so hard to commit to paper. This is *not* to say that I write line-by-line comments or copious notes at the end of each entry. It didn't take me long to figure the math on that: if each student writes, say, sixteen entries a grading period, and I'm writing extensive comments on each page, and there are seventy student journals to review, I'm writing long comments on over a thousand pieces of paper. *Impossible.*

Instead, I write *very* quick comments in the margins. Some are empathetic: *Oh, no!* Some are exclamatory: *Wow!* Others are direct response to information: *I didn't know that!* Others are brief praise: *Great writing here!* and still others are more in the category of *sound* than semantics: *Yecchh!* Sometimes, of course—especially when a student asks you a direct question in the journal—the response is longer, and very specific.

Are any of the short responses "critical"? Sometimes. I'll often write in the margin, *I'm having a hard time reading this, George,* or *This is impossible to read!* or *George! Remember our protocol on margins!* (often quickly sketching out the proper margins with my pen), or *Hey! Where's the paragraphing?*

Especially during the first grading period's read, I make an attempt to have at least *some* comments on each entry. On some pages there's only one comment; on some there are many.

All these comments, largely positive, let the students know that, indeed, you have given *your* time to the time that *they* have so respectfully and laboriously given over to their journals. In their totality, kids are impressed. But, clearly, short comments in margins are not enough: students need a more comprehensive assessment.

## THE INSIDE FRONT COVER: THE GRADE AND THE *TEACHER'S* WRITING

You've read "Vanessa's" journal now, from the front page of the stapled sheaf to the back. You've made comments in the margins and occasional quick comments at the tops of papers or at ends of entries. You've even responded quickly in some length to an issue she felt passionately about in an entry. Now you're ready first to evaluate it for a grade, then to make important summative comments.

Using the protocol you established with the kids weeks ago, you assess the journal for its grade, *based strictly on length.*

You flip through, noticing carefully whether Vanessa paid heed to the "one thumb" margin rule (jeez, if it's a *finger* or slightly *more* than a thumb, no big deal!), whether she pulled one of those five-words-a-line tricks, her cursive so large you could pass a giant crochet hook through the loops, or skipped double lines between paragraphs, or indented six inches, or started each entry far down on the page, or actually *switched paper on you* and substituted wide-rule, or any other of the ingenious and admirable tricks that so faithfully reflect kids' creativity.

If any of these things occurred, you take gentle mental note.

Next, you thumb through the pages quickly, one by one, keeping track of how much Vanessa has written. Maybe the first day she filled half of a front sheet. You'll have a "C" in mind to start. Then, two more pages in which she reached the end of each. She's pulling her average up: it's looking like a "B-." Now, for most of the remaining dozen, she's really "cranked it up," and consistently has written five or six lines on the other side of the page. Great! She's got herself an "A-."

The patterns are fairly clear; you get good at evaluating how much a student has written. (Once in a while, certainly, you'll need to thumb through a *few* times to ascertain your accuracy.)

What you *don't* take into consideration for the grade:

- Neatness *(though in your comments you'll express disappointment about difficulties you had in deciphering a journal)*

- Spelling

- Grammar or syntax

- Diction (use and choice of words)

- Second-language issues

- Subject matter, unless it's the legislated-against "I woke up at 7:00, etc." repetition
- Whether the student wrote or did not write on the prompt
- Whether a goodly number of journals are "private" *(though for this first round, should you encounter lots of private journals, you'll exhort the writers not to have so many private entries next time, explaining that they "lock you out," and you can't get access to their writing skills)*
- Whether the student has driven you crazy during Journal Time, having signaled to you a hundred times that grading period with questions you deemed superfluous

For students, the thrust of Fluency Journals is all about length, and your good judgment on a student's production will rarely be challenged.

## MORE ON THE CARROT AND STICK

Grading Fluency Journals is not a precise science, but as year by year you read hundreds of journals, you'll become more confident that your grades are fair.

We've spoken earlier of reasons to delay beginning the Fluency Journals until about the fourth week of instruction: the snowstorm of paperwork during the first weeks, much student transition between classes, and important details such as getting to know the kids' names.

There's another reason. By the fourth week, you usually know your kids' skill levels. You've reviewed their scores on the (arguably valuable) standardized tests, you've given them assessments of your own, you've worked with them and watched them in (in?)action, and you've received, read, noticed, and responded to some of their work. Therefore you've got a good idea not only of their capabilities but of the concomitant effort they're exerting.

It's these at least partly understood students to whom you're speaking in that fourth week—students who are beginning to understand that you understand their work, and who are beginning to know that you know them, even if only in a limited way.

So when the day arrives for you to collect the journals and take them home— usually six to eight weeks into the semester—you're beginning to know the kids fairly well. You see the students' faces as you're reading their journals, you know each one's skills and abilities in your subject matter, and you know the history of their work.

What does this mean for me, when I read, for the first round, my students' Fluency Journals? It means that I keep my word on the manner in which I grade: an average of half a page of writing gets a "C," and average of a full side gets a "B," and an average of three or four lines on the back gets an "A."

*But.* But, as you know, there are grades that could go either way: a "B-" could be a "C" in some cases, and a "B+" could be an "A." And that's when knowing the kids comes into play. If Vanessa, for example, seems, by my weeks of observation, to be lazing a bit during Journal Time, or if Hugo, who normally works at a slow pace, seems verily *burning* through his journals, writing all the way, those observations can throw the grade in either direction during this first grading period. *I've found, for those close cases, that grading on the "low" end of the spectrum during the first grading period gets results.* Usually this first, lower grade is given with an exhortative explanation:

*1st Quarter Grade: C+. Vanessa! You were so close to a "B"! This journal was terrific and detailed in so many places, and full of lots of fresh insights and ideas. Next time, be sure to write at least six or seven lines more, and you'll assure yourself of a "B." (Why not go for an "A," while you're at it?)*

This, then, serves less as stick-as-cudgel, and more as that carrot-shaped stick, fern-like at its head, root-like at its tip, urging the student along. (All right, I promise: enough of the vegetative imagery.)

During subsequent grading periods, I tend to "curve upward," and grade on the generous end, sometimes mentioning in the comments that "this 'B' is a little gift— an investment in the future of *more* writing, right, Vanessa?"

Now, let's discuss further the two ends of the grading spectrum.

At one end of the grading spectrum is the student who has performed spectacularly. As a teacher, why not get excited? You've had a good read, the student has done *more* than you required, showing an often astounding passion for the work. I often give "A+'s" in journals, and admit to, rather regularly, in celebratory joy, giving "A++'s." Why not? Accompanied by a sincerely enthusiastic note (see "Examples of Comments" later in this chapter), you're almost certain to have locked in such stellar performance for the year, and a cadre of exemplary writers whose concentrated energy has a profound influence on the atmosphere of the class during Journal Time.

Alas, though, we teachers know that some students will be at the opposite end of the spectrum, and here I'm not referring to "special situation" students discussed later. These are mainstream students who possess at least moderate skills—you've seen evidence of them, both in test scores and, at least sporadically, in other work in your class. You've seen them put out accurate work, and even some instances of adequately developed writing.

These (few, usually *very* few) are simply not taking the journal process seriously and have squandered many twenty-minute periods, producing each time a few sloppy lines of unfocused, lethargic prose.

What to do? First, obviously, *notice* what's going on before the end of the grading period, when the cumulative effect of their lassitude can lower their grade. (See "Frozen Writers Counseling" in Chapter Eight.) Try to intervene, using a few different strategies—strategies including direct, whispered remonstrations.

Still, little work? You know your student: might he or she respond, during this first grading period, to the shock of a *very* low grade and an accompanying excoriative comment? (Again, see examples that follow.) I've had very good results from such: actually giving a low "C" or a rare "D" or (even rarer) "D-," and a serious, direct, no-nonsense, lengthy comment. Confronted with the combination of low grade and stern teacher concern, the student—especially one who respects the teacher as someone who's generally honest and fair—often acts quickly to do better.

The psychology's complex here, and we as teachers know best whether a student will respond best to excoriation or gentle goading. Fortunately, these extreme situations are the exception, not the rule, and the entire grading process usually presents few such quandaries.

## WRITING SUMMATIVE COMMENTS

It's one thing to assign a grade. Given the system under which we labor, students *do* want a grade on their work, and we're responsible for giving them one.

But grades are clinical, and what kids *really* want is our human response: our thoughts and feelings about the writing into which they've poured so much energy. They want a little guidance—not a lot, for a lot can easily overwhelm—and a perception of appreciation. They're new writers, remember, and they want to have a sense of whether their words are succeeding—primarily in communicating in the language, and secondarily in persuading or painting the picture or interpreting or making you laugh or communicating grief or despair or passion or exultation or any of the myriad reasons writers put pen to paper. Perhaps, they may worry, their words are falling into the bottomless well of so much of their school writing, never to be retrieved.

Therefore it seems important, along with the brief comments you've already sprinkled liberally through their entries, to write a single, overarching summative comment just below their grade on the inside front cover of the journal folder.

I usually write a paragraph—usually short, sometimes long. Rather than go into an exegesis of the nature and philosophy of these comments, let's simply share some real comments from the last two years' student journals (see the exhibit that follows on pp. 106–107). Included are relatively effusive comments, middling comments, and a few moderately disapproving ones. (Remember that these summative comments are in tandem with terse comments written on the journal entries themselves. A taxonomy of those can be found in Appendix C.)

You get the picture: cheerleading is important here, occasional pointed (and brief!) format, style, and grammatical therapy can have an audience, and, for the salvation of the teacher reading many journals, brevity can sometimes yield more rewards than an (often unread) page full of corrective prose.


## SUBSEQUENT GRADING

During the second grading period—in our school the second quarter of the semester, ending mid-January, I read journals the same way I read them the first time around: quickly word-for-word, often skimming, but looking carefully at each page. My commentary remains the same. (I actually enjoy the second grading period "reads" a little better; I tend to read a few journals a day during Winter Break and find that a new affection builds for the kids over the holidays. Don't get me wrong: we all desperately need the psychological break of time off—it's just that I don't return too demoralized, and I think the journals help that.)

Let's say we're three-quarters through the year now, and the journal process is continuing apace, running well. The *kids* have hit that relaxed homeostasis that occurs mid-year, the curriculum hums, but for me, around March, there are so many demands that I feel as if I've been thrust—along with my colleagues—into a linear accelerator. Everything speeds up, "free" time shrinks, and I find that *fully* reading the journals becomes exceedingly difficult. I've looked at the phenomenon carefully, and it occurs every year.

How to handle this? I've tried a few things. Two or three years I knuckled down, put all other work aside, and read. That worked for the journals, but other teaching duties and preparation suffered.

## Summative Comments: What They Look Like

Here are some sample summative comments from Fluency Journals over the past two years. Of course, your own diction will be different, and your students will respond to your voice:

A++     Lisa, this journal is a teacher's dream. It's wise, funny, fluent, topical (*even* when you chastise the teacher!) and wonderful in every way. Keep up the *great* work!

A+     Wow, what a wonderful journal, Rachelle. I enjoyed reading it. You're a lively writer: very skilled. You *really* wrote an engaging, powerful (often sad!) journal, and one that you'll look back on one day with pride. I look forward to the next.

A+     What a fantastic journal, Samantha. Smart, funny, full of feeling, *very* impressive. Keep it up!

A     A terrific journal, Edgar: witty, wise, wordy. Next time, *paragraphs*, eh? You're driving me crazy! (Looking forward to the next read.)

B     Bobby—This journal—wacky as it is—probably saved you from an "F" in my class. Keep up the long writing next time, and do try to write on the topic sometimes!

B     Maybe could have been close to a "B+," but those huge margins worked against you, Vanessa. Overall, though, a *wonderful* journal, V. *Lots* of fun for a teacher to read. Your writing is engaging and skilled. Keep it up! (Watch those margins!)

B     Bock, this is a fine journal. You are both a skilled writer and a sophisticated thinker. Keep up the good work. Fix those margins, write a little bigger to help an old man's eyes, and go longer—you're close to an "A."

B–     Louis—an interesting journal read—but I think you can write *much more next time* (and try to "stretch your wings" by using some new words this time, OK? Vocab here a little basic...)

B–     Some *great* entries, some very weak ones, Theresa. I want you to try harder next time, and raise this grade. There's no reason you can't; you're a good writer.

**B−**  Lynn—I enjoyed reading this but must say I was a little disappointed: partly, of course, in its length, but partly because I consider you a deep thinker and didn't see you going into much *depth* yet. I hope to see/read more of that smart, deep *self* next time! (Feels like not *lots* of effort/energy here.)

**C+**  A decent start, Sutdan. For next time remember 1) pen, 2) paragraphs, and 3) more writing! You can *easily* get an "A" or "B" in journal—Your ideas come fast and are fun to read.

**C+**  Brian—This was a hard journal to grade. All those huge spaces between tiny words. Next time, please: 1) paragraphs, 2) pen, 3) write larger, and 4) no big gaps between words, OK?

**C+**  Dennis—I feel as if you did the minimum—wide margins when I cautioned you against them, lots of repeating/rephrasing the prompts (which is OK *sometimes*), but very little of *your* thinking, eh? I look forward to the next reading.

**C**  You may be surprised at the grade, Robert. Next time: 1) follow the rules about *titles, dates,* and *margins,* and 2) get many more words on each line by writing smaller. I know you'll get a good grade next time if you do these things and write more.

**C**  OK, Anita. You've got a lot of work to do. 1) Present papers neatly, 2) write so that I can read your words, 3) put titles on your entries, and 4) write a *date*. I *know* you'll raise your grade next time!

**C**  Jim, this "C" was a gift. I finally gave up—tired of reading light *pencil* and words I could hardly make out. I *know* you were there when I went over journal protocol and explained what I wanted: 1) *ink,* 2) *titles,* 3) *dates,* 4) *writing neat enough for me to read,* and 5) *paragraphing.* Now get going—this stuff will never fly in high school!

**D**  A disaster, Mike. I expect lots more writing next time. *You can do it,* and I'm confident in you. We need to talk about this.

Here's what I often do now. At the end of the third grading period, the students having written madly in their journals twice a week, I ask students to identify the *eight* journal entries they want me to read. I tell them that I'll still be grading them *all* on the basis of achieved length, but will only read eight.

At first, I felt that I was cheating the kids in this method. But what I found—and I hope that this isn't an elaborate rationalization—is that students take a real sense of challenge in evaluating the journals they want me to look at, and that their choices are wise and keen.

I expected complaints from this process—"Hey! We're doing all this writing, and you're only reading half of it!"—but none materialized. What I learned was that, at mid-year, the Fluency Journals have become ingrained in the best sense of that word: they serve not the teacher but the self, and are regarded almost utterly as self-exploration and self-development. The teacher, though important as guide, is becoming tangential.

In the final grading period, something else tends to occur: massive end-of-year interruption. You know the scene: standardized tests, special assemblies, track championships, visits from guest speakers or counselors, performances, ad infinitum. It's really hard to pull off twice-a-week Fluency Journals, and I'll usually pull the program down to once per week. (Yes, there are complaints, but yes, there is other curriculum that must be taught, part of which includes full-bodied essay work that uses the mental "muscles" developed during Fluency Journal work throughout the year.)

In this final grading period, then, there are fewer journal entries to read. I give them a good read, comment as usual, grade them, and make a year-end "summary-summary" comment as a good-bye.

## GRADING FOR SPECIAL SITUATIONS

I say *special situations* because most of what you'll see and evaluate in regard to length is pretty clear-cut. And I can report to you that only one or two times in many years have students questioned a grade they received.

But a few issues do pop up and must be grappled with. And grappling it is, in some cases.

• *What about kids who write eight words on a typical line and other kids who write six words on a line?* Is it not fair to give that eight-word kid a little extra boost? Absolutely. As suggested earlier, there are plenty of "gray areas" and "round off upward or round off downward" areas in the process: it's not trigonometry. And there are, indeed, students who write in extremely small cursive, cramming lots of words on a line. Of course, I tend to round their grades considerably upward. (Curiously, I find that those many-words-on-a-line students often tend to rise to the occasion and produce "A" length work no matter what their cursive habits are.)

• *What about Special Education students?* It occurs frequently in schools that an English class contains Special Education students whose skills in the subject matter might be quite low. What to do with such students, when the standard that must be reached for a grade—which you've announced and shown examples that reflect it—is difficult for them to achieve? This is a subject about which entire books have been written, but I'll tell you what I do, and as a professional you can make your own judgment.

First, I don't assume that Special Ed students—even if they've tested low in the language arts—can't write prolifically. Even if their early attempts at writing in other arenas in your class have resulted in paltry output, I still involve them as fully fledged class members in what I expect. I've learned that it's often premature to preempt Special Education students with an offer of remediation of the standard when they may not want that at all and may rise to the occasion—especially when they witness the energetic, intense writing going on in class.

Second, *for the first grading period* I grade them the same as the rest of the students. Unless a student completely flouts the journal activity, writing only a line or so a day then "kicking back" for the rest of the writing time (this is rare), I usually don't give a grade lower than a "C–." Truly, it is quite difficult to get below a "C," which asks for only half of the front sheet written on, usually containing a single paragraph or two.

After that first grading period, I'm often surprised that Special Education kids have written far more than I might have expected. In those cases, I'm effusive with comments on the inside front cover: lots of exclamation marks and deserved praise. If, however, it's clear that the student is struggling, I'll suggest in my note that we meet and talk. The talk is usually outside class time; that way, the student is not singled out during class: such a "pull-aside" can be embarrassing for kids.

The conversation goes something like this. You open "Roger's" journal:
*Roger, are you having a tough time with your journal?*
"Uh, yeah, I guess so."
*What's been hard for you?*
"Uh, writing a lot. It's hard to write a lot. I don't know what to say."

*Well, you may have gotten a "C," but you're doing pretty well. I* do *notice that you work at it for the whole twenty minutes, don't you?*

"Yeah, mostly."

*What if we worked out a deal—just between us. You try to average just* four *more lines this next grading period, and we'll crank that grade up to a "B," OK? Do you think you might be able to do it?*

"Uh, maybe I can. I'll try."

Roger smiles a little. He thinks he can do it.

You've raised the bar, but haven't placed it so high that Roger doesn't feel that he can't get a running jump at it.

And most often, he does jump it, for which you reward him with that "B," and talk with him again—even if only quickly as you pass in the hall—and suggest that he try during the *next* grading period to get to the *bottom* of the page for an "A."

Yes, it's capitalist—the whole grading system is capitalist—and no, it's not quite "fair" to the mass of other students. But it works. If Roger's attitude is defeated and bitter he won't—in your class, at least—become a better writer. But the other pole exists, too: that in your class Roger discovered that he not only does not hate writing, he *can* write with a measure of competence.

• *What about English language learners?* The same is true for them. They struggle similarly, perhaps fluent in writing their native language, or perhaps uneducated even in their native country. Whatever describes them, the specter of not only understanding the prompt but synthesizing it and then meeting the goal of many written words can overwhelm them.

What to do? The Roger model, honey rather than vinegar. (I *did* promise to get away from that vegetable motif.) A quick personal talk, a little encouragement, the setting of an *achievable goal,* and the continued, low-key goading toward expanded fluency in our new, strange language.

In both Roger's case and that of the English-language learner, it's clear that each is more afraid of committing errors than a "mainstream" student would be. It's important to reemphasize to these students the fact that you're not worried about spelling or grammatical correctness in the Fluency Journals. (*Spell as well as you can, and write as well as you can, but just try to* get it down *while you're thinking of things.*) This needs reinforcement throughout the year. Further, I've noticed that with these students there's often a kind of disconnective, interruptive static among the *reading* of the concepts of the prompt (and processing it), the *writing* about it, and the whole idea that it's not only acceptable but desirable to put down on paper what's in one's mind. In Roger's case, he's often been exposed only to rote work, and, therefore, the relative freedom—and demands implicit in that freedom—panic him a little. In the case of English language learners, they, too, may be unaccustomed to the frank topics optionally written about, and they may often share Roger's paralysis in this new freedom. (It's been my experience that when English language learners do attain confidence, it builds quickly, and they frequently and stunningly break loose in the Fluency Journals, much to their own delight—and mine!)

## ALTERNATIVE EVALUATION PRACTICES

The assessment and grading process you just read is what I put into place in my own classroom: a mixed-ability urban eighth-grade class whose population rarely falls below twenty-eight and often reaches thirty-six. However, readers of this book will not necessarily have classes that reflect either that demographic or those numbers.

Other ways of assessing and grading the Fluency Journals certainly are possible. Some of them are a little painful for me to write about, because they involve very small class sizes—something I may never experience during my teaching career. They're more human and personal. Here are some ideas:

- For very small classes, the possibility of reading students' Fluency Journals *every day* is very conceivable. This would deeply increase the sense of connection between writer and teacher. Teachers would even be able to sneak in a few personally tailored syntax and grammar lessons without "poisoning the well" with didactic and off-putting "corrections."

- Under certain conditions—for example, in working with a highly skilled, highly motivated, probably small group—I can imagine not "grading" the journals at all: simply pursuing the above-mentioned commentary process and *skipping* the grade, rigorously *assuming* that all kids will participate fully. The "grade" can simply translate into class participation and be integrated into the final assessment in any way the teacher desires. (A caveat here, though: should this method be used, the danger is that Journal Time could degenerate into the journal process used so widely in schools today: a rambling, unfocused dissipater of time.)

- Some teachers, again with smaller classes, might prefer grading more frequently so as to move their students more quickly toward the gradual extension of written fluency.

- Meredith has suggested that once the program is "up and running" students might sometimes be asked to *grade themselves.* This seems a great idea to me, and I intend to try it. On my part, I imagine pursuing such a self-grading experiment during the *second* semester, when the protocols are not only in place, but second nature. (And why not, accompanying the grade, ask each student to write a reflective *comment* accompanying *your* evaluative comment? I can imagine the student comment coming either *in response* to the teacher's words or *first,* and the teacher responding to the student's thoughts.) This grade-yourself process wouldn't function to save the teacher much time: thumbing through the pages to give an overall grade is not too time-consuming—but its self-analytical aspect certainly recommends it. And students *still* would want their teacher's comments.

- You could also, with the right class, have the students experiment with grading one another's work. A great by-product here would be that writers would be exposed to *other* writers' journal work, and get some new rhetorical ideas.

# Extending the Work

The Fluency Journal process described in this book is certainly "enough" in the curricular sense: there's plenty there for both student and teacher without further embellishment.

However, it's useful to say a few words about *sharing*—a process we humans like to engage in—and extending into other areas the work kids have done. Neither needs to be complicated, and I've chosen here to include only activities that have proved to work.

## WAYS TO SHARE JOURNALS

I've discussed the importance of the Fluency Journals' privacy. They're put away in a file cabinet or other closed area, unavailable to students who might think of picking them up. They're distributed and collected by the same trusted, reliable student all semester or all year. The teacher doesn't leave them around the classroom while in the process of reviewing them over a day's or two days' time. They're *safe,* and if that safety is compromised, student trust in the process disintegrates.

However, sometimes students *want* to share their journals: either in toto with other students or with the class, orally. When that energy is evident and expressed, you know you've taken another victory toward solidifying the Fluency Journal as a lodestone in your class—it's a magnetic identifier now, and will be permanent.

It's worth thinking about ways to approach the oral reading of journals. That's constantly important—the time it takes is its primary "problem"—and those ideas remain in play here. (We should have such problems! That kids are proud of their work and want to read it!) But there are other strategies, too, that keep interest keen. I'll list and comment briefly on ways of sharing that have worked for me:

• Sharing the day's entry with another student or group of students. The teacher announces ahead of time, *Today's a day when we'll be sharing what we write. Not anything in your journal: just what you write today. So keep that in mind when you're writing, you guys!* Those days I'll usually choose a high-interest, sometimes goofy prompt that would make the sharing process safe and not too personal.

At the end of Journal Time (I usually run these sessions for fifteen instead of twenty minutes), students choose one other student with whom to share their entries. (Clearly, if there is an odd "three" at the end, or a loner student who doesn't have a partner in the class with whom to share, the teacher will vigilantly anticipate such and become the quiet matchmaker.)

*After you've read your partner's journal,* I'll say, *write a comment at the end of it. Say what you liked about it. Be specific. Underline the words, if you want. Make any other comments you want, as long as they're respectful and polite!*

This is fun, done occasionally. It keeps investment in the project at a high level.

• Announcing that today's journal will be a letter to someone in the class. *But.* But not a social letter: a letter on a controversial issue. The day's prompt might be about the death penalty, or abortion, or the current war that we're involved in, or other topics ripe for polemics. Students are told that today's journal prompt is mandatory. They choose a partner (my earlier comment about teacher-as-matchmaker is still relevant, of course) and write, as their journal entry, a letter *to* that partner on the subject. *They must take a stand,* advocate a side, even if they're ambivalent on the subject.

Journals are exchanged, read, and there are a few ways to go here: either have each student write a response on the spot—this works well—or have the students each *take their partner's journal entry home* and return the next day with a response. (If you teach in an area with fulminating fundamentalist parents, it's conceivable that this last device could cause both you and your student trouble, so use your best judgment—the old "choose your battles" dictum—in assigning this as an activity.)

• A pass-around. Again, make an announcement *before* the prompt is read. *OK, everybody. I want to let you know that* today, *and* today only, *we're going to be passing our journal entries around the class. So please know that you classmates will be* seeing *today's writing, and adjust it in any way you need to.* Ask kids to write their names on today's paper; they're not accustomed to doing that.

So students write, and when "time" is called, begin a quick "pass-around" *of that day's papers only,* clockwise through the room, perhaps using a timer, limiting the amount of time for reading to, say, two minutes per entry. The timer goes off, the teacher says, *OK—pass!* And the rotation continues.

This is the "read-only" model of this idea. A variation is to ask *each* student to make *one* comment (again, politeness legislated) on the paper before passing it on. A little more time, of course, needs to be allowed for this version of the pass-around. By the end of class, then, even if not every student has gotten a chance to read each entry, all the returning papers have lots of interesting comments for the author to read. (I feel strongly that the teacher ought to be in the class group, acting as both timekeeper and reader and commenter.)

## EXPLORING OTHER CONTENT AREAS

Many extensions are possible in the Fluency Journal process, limited, perhaps, only by time factors and the teacher's imagination. Here are a few that have worked for me:

• Mandatory prompts exploring literature or social studies: Assuming that yours is not simply a writing class but a general English class, consider extending the Fluency Journal process *very occasionally* to include a prompt that resonates from a particular literary work you're reading. For example, John Proctor's struggle in *The Crucible* is a perfect journal-prompt-in-waiting. Why not structure a *Crucible* prompt in the manner of the usual prompts, and ask kids to write on *it?* The kids will bring that "journal energy" into the prompt, and you'll be fulfilling any one of numerous state standards under the rubric of "response to literature."

Some of us also teach social studies—either to the same group or to others. The journal process is *perfect* for response to social studies issues. Again, a prompt might have to do with Washington's role as hero in the Revolutionary War, or Dr. Martin Luther King's struggle as embattled hero during the Chicago march. If the prompt is structured similarly—the larger question leading off, questions within questions within—a prompt is easily made, and kids are accustomed to writing fluently from it.

(And guess what? Don't tell the kids this, but they've just written, in twenty or so minutes, a sophisticated first draft for an essay. Keep that a secret—seriously!—or it will alter the students' attitude toward the journals.)

*—I do worry about too many "extensions," and for good reason. I use them seldom during the year, having found that if kids get the sense that the journals are a ruse used by the teachers to wheedle essays out of them, they'll feel less proprietary, feel less sense of control over their journals, and the energy will slowly leak away until the journals are worthless drudgery. So if you use extensions at all, please use them judiciously.*

## POSSIBLE MODIFICATIONS TO THE PROGRAM

Having developed the Fluency Journal program over many years, certainly I'd assert that what's been presented here is the optimum way to run the program.

However, let's talk about alterations—those that work and those that don't.

• *Going shorter, going longer:* The Fluency Journal program *can* work using a fifteen-minute basis rather than twenty. You'll get less writing, obviously, and will have to adjust your grading scale accordingly. But if you have a fairly resistant class, or a particularly low-skilled—even nonnative-speaker—class, you might begin this way during the first semester. (In regular classes, however, I've found that it often takes kids ten minutes just to get their writing and thinking self-rolling, and that the prose generated in the last ten minutes often contains the most distinctive voice and most interesting writing. Further, as the months move on, if you're like me, you'll find *many* kids raising their hands when you occasionally ask that "Who needs more time?" question. That's a good sign: committed writing going on, a zeal to excel. Why cut it off early?)

Conversely, the idea of longer journal-time can take kids great places in their writing. Kids will welcome the idea of, say, thirty minutes rather than twenty. If you embark upon this course, though, two things are essential: first, that all kids "buy in" to the extension and are on task, and second, that you as a teacher are giving kids personal feedback on their writing more quickly than in the usual program. Kids will not sustain such extended writing time without quick feedback. (I can envision private schools or rare public schools with very small class sizes embracing this extended model.)

The downside? Two days a week wherein almost the entire period is devoted to Fluency Journals. In my own situation, I grieve that I can't afford the time, but that's the reality: there's literature and syntax and spelling and vocabulary and other kinds of writing on which to focus. (Is yours specifically a writing class? Terrific! I'd jump at the chance for such an extended program, then.)

• *Using Fluency Journals only one day a week:* Yes, the program described in this book asks for two days per week, about half an hour per day. The reality, though, is that every school has its interruptions: assemblies, fire drills, hearing and vision tests, special visits by speakers who can only arrange to come on the day you're normally doing journals, and so on. So the two-day a week regimen *does* get interrupted with some frequency in the normal course of school business.

Going formally to one day a week *is* possible—I've tried it in the past—but that alteration comes with some observations and exhortations. First, I've noticed that after a few weeks of a one-day-a-week regimen, students really slow down in their writing, as if they're getting "rusty." And I've noticed that unless the teacher energizes the program "cheerleaderishly," its vigor flags. If you do decide to try a one-day-a-week regimen, I'd exhort you to adopt that during the *second* semester, when the program is well-inculcated into your classroom's writing psyche, and consider doing the thirty-minute model rather than twenty.

• *Increasing the frequency to three or four times per week:* I'm not absolutely certain of many things in life, but of this I am: any more than twice a week will exterminate the program's energy within three weeks. (*Wouldn't it be a good idea to do it for three weeks and then quit? Wouldn't I get lots of writing in that three-week period?*) Sure, you'd get lots of writing in a short period, but the kids won't have a chance to get their "writer's legs," to relax in the routine, to range across topics, explore ideas, play with voice.

• *Doing the journals intensively—say, for thirty-minute sessions—twice a week for one semester only:* Sure! That would work. In my own practice I do the entire

—*What about choosing to do journals twice a week, as normal, but allowing the days to "float," fitting into your schedule as you like it? I tried that one semester, and the kids did not take well to it. Too unpredictable for them: they wanted—even were comforted by—the routine of Tuesday and Thursday.*

year, and find that kids get testy—a similar testiness to that which comes when a musician doesn't play for a while, a painter doesn't paint for a while—if they don't get to their journals. But there's nothing inherent in the one-semester idea that will co-opt the Fluency Journal program in any fundamental way.

• *Having the kids write in spiral-bound notebooks, instead of the decorated manila folders holding loose-leaf paper:* I can only report to you what I've found. The first idea is that the self-decorated folders have meaning for kids, even if we teachers don't understand that meaning or think the folders sometimes look a little eccentric—that *personalization* issue that seems very powerful. It's pretty difficult to "go artsy" on spiral-bound notebooks. The second bit of information is that, when Meredith and I broached this idea with a class—the same class that nearly threw tomatoes at us when we suggested preprinted rather than hand-at-board-scripted prompts—they *loathed* the idea, and claimed it would take the fun out of the process. *We have those notebooks so much,* they said—*math, science, God, we've had them all our lives!*

It was *very* clear that consigning Fluency Journals to spiral notebooks or binders would be like sending their energy to some federal penitentiary, and the program would become another "drill," devoid of individuality.

• *Quitting the music a few sessions before the end of the year:* A colleague and I discussed this idea, and I'll be experimenting with it this year. The rationale: when students leave your class and enter another next year, they'll need to take the fluency skills they've gained with them. But that fluency this year often arrived concomitant with music, and chances are that most writing they'll do for the remainder of their scholarly careers will *not* be accompanied by music. So, in the interest of not unleashing hordes of students into the "big world" (wherever that place is) who are only able to write passionately and volubly when they're hearing excellent music, it seems that a "weaning" process might be indicated—say, a few weeks at the end wherein all other aspects (prompts, quiet, expectations) remain in place, but the music, perhaps to their chagrin, is absent.

I've little doubt that, after a few vocalized complaints, students immersed year-round in the Fluency Journal process will rise to the silent occasion, write, and write well.

# Au Revoir, Journals!

Look ahead to the end of the year: It's been quite an effort.

When the year began, you carefully and energetically went through, with the kids, the step-by-step protocol of Fluency Journals. For their part, they were respectful, yet nonetheless had that glazed *I can never possibly do this* look in their eyes. (And was there a hidden tentativeness on your part—the teacher who, though speaking authoritatively and emphatically, wondered, below the bravado, whether the whole thing would work?)

That's all behind you now, on this last day of Fluency Journals, when you've perhaps given that "Last Journal" prompt and maybe even devoted the entire period to kids' readings, discussions of the journals' joys and despairs, "favorite prompt" and "strangest prompt" awards, and a general synthesizing and evaluating of the entire process.

Notice today how the kids handle their journals. Certainly, there will be a few who don't care much for them: never did. But the great majority of kids handle them almost tenderly, shuffling through during your discussion to recall what they'd written, to bring back the wash of those feelings, those passions, those cognitive connections made.

It seems a good idea, now that we're evaluating, for the teacher to *go specific,* asking questions about not just content but *improvement:* the nameable progress made, asking the class, *How many kids were able to write longer entries as the year progressed? How many kids found themselves using fancier vocabulary, taking a chance on new words? How many kids learned more about* conventions—*spelling and grammar and structure?* Questions like that.

On the last day, I often go into a little speech urging kids not simply to take their journals home and put them somewhere carelessly, perhaps to be thrown away by a parent or sibling. *Hang onto these, everybody. When you read them again in ten years, twenty years, you'll learn a lot about yourself. You'll say, "Hey! I was a pretty thoughtful person!" Or, "Hey! I've changed so much since then! But still, this is darned good writing, and I was aware of lots of important issues!"*

I can tell you that over the years I've often had former students return to visit and speak of the journals as a "special time," reporting that they still pick up their journal occasionally and read it. And, as important to me as a teacher, many report that the Fluency Journals "broke loose" their writing, and that writing in subsequent years came much easier for their having had the Fluency Journals experience.

The overwhelming sense I get in these visits is a nostalgia for the time we spent together twice a week—with that intensive focus, the music asserting itself into their writers' psyches, the prompts offering respect for their thoughts and their lives, and the deep, sustained quiet: a quiet unavailable to so many of them.

Finally, a last little physical detail: remember the binder paper that was all of the same stock and size? There was a reason! Punch holes in the journal folders, have kids ceremonially "bind" them through the lined-up holes with fancy yarn or ribbon, give them a large manila envelope in which to carry (conceal?) them, and send kids and journals home.

*Bon voyage,* journals: get ye safely home.

---

*I'm very proud of my journal.
It's a book of my thoughts.*

---

—George Zhu

---

*I found that I enjoyed writing more than
I thought I did. Since I did so much journal
writing, I found that I love to write.*

---

—Elena Escalante

**PART FOUR**

# The Prompts

The writing prompts you'll find in this section are numbered and grouped by category, but in no particular order. Each number is accompanied by a "quick topic key" that identifies its subject to assist busy teachers in their twice-weekly search. (Clearly, there's no need to put either the number or the title on the board; kids' own [often creative] titling process will be discouraged if a title is already in place for them.) Emphasized words in the prompts are underlined, rather than italicized, because teachers will be underlining them on the board.

A few other notes. First, as mentioned earlier, it's really important to alternate the diet of prompts. That is, a program in which kids arrive each day to see rather lighthearted or trivial prompts would soon lose its sense of fundamental seriousness; conversely, if students arrived each day to see only heavy, soul-searching prompts, Journal Time might become too grim for them, and they'd come to dread it. A graceful alternation seems appropriate. Second, I think it's best not to assume that only middle-school kids would respond to the lighthearted and imaginative ones and that only high-school kids would respond to the deeper, soul-searching, philosophical ones. Not true: each group goes for each, and, I'd argue, needs each.

Some of the prompts are quite similar and are provided to offer choice in variation. Others, though similar, reflect shades of meaning that will yield distinctly different writing.

Finally, my own bias, certainly, is that the prompts be used fully, for editing or shortening would tend to eliminate doors through which kids can enter a prompt, or eliminate specificities onto which they can hang paragraphs.

## PROMPT TOPICS

This list is for your convenience. As noted, the titles themselves are not written on the board; it works better to give students an opportunity to generate their own focus and choose their own title.

### First Day

1. First Journal Entry

### Relationships

2. Defining a Good Friend

3. Betrayal

4. Hurt Feelings—Intentional or Not

5. Crushes

6. Making Friends

7. Friends, in Number

8. Ulterior Motives

9. Lending and Borrowing

10. Friends of Opposite Sex

11. Long Overdue Letter

12. Dislikes: People

13. Change: Personal Development

14. Major Life-Changes

15. Boys' Relationships with Boys, Girls' with Girls

16. Differences Between Boys and Girls

17. Relationship with Telephone

18. Arguments: Causes

19. Strategies for Avoiding Conflicts

20. Advice to Adults: How to Communicate with Kids

21. Kids' Version of House Rules

22. Switch Roles Day

50. Noticing Drivers' Behavior

51. Enough Vacation Time in U.S.?

52. Boys'/Girls' Treatment in School

53. Undeserved Trouble

54. Rudeness Defined

55. Clichés

56. U.S. as World Leader

57. "State of Union"

58. Importance of Money

59. Relative Importance of Jobs

## Goofy and Imaginative

60. Sudden Ability to Fly

61. Sudden Invisibility

62. Power to See Underwater

63. Choose or Create Own Superhero

64. Healing Touch

65. One Super Power

66. Unlimited Travel

67. Sudden Superstar

68. Celebrity Falls in Love with You

69. Spend $200

70. Solve Two Problems

71. Everyone Imitates You

72. Love Potion

73. Trickster

## The Natural World

74. Rainy Days

75. Windy Days

76. Rodent Attitude

77. Insect Attitude

78. Attention to Birds

79. Thinking About the Cosmos

80. Balance of Nature

81. Favorite Water Form

82. Underground Imaginings

83. Careful Observations

84. Build an Animal

85. Improve on Nature

## Taking Risks; Aspirations

86. Risks Taken

87. Survival Strategies

88. What Sort of Adult to Be?

89. Risks to Be Taken

90. Future Career Thoughts

91. A Moment When Everything Changed

92. How Do You Best Learn?

93. Earliest Memory

94. Aspirations Mocked

95. What Are You Good at?

## Inventions, Innovations, and Pastimes

96. Invent a Board Game

97. Invent a Sport

98. Invent a Video Game

## Dreams

## Deep Life Issues

## Last Day

## FIRST DAY

### 1. (First Journal Entry)

Have you written in journals before, either at home or in school?

What was the nature of your writing: was it on particular subjects, or was it simply "freewrites," wherein you wrote what you felt like writing?

If you had journals in school, how did the teacher structure them? Were you satisfied with the process? Did you feel as if you did well, or were you unsatisfied?

And what about this journal process this year? Are you feeling a little overwhelmed, or are you confident? Are you eager to write about lots of things, or are you anxious (nervous)?

Write about journals today.

## RELATIONSHIPS

### 2. (Defining a Good Friend)

What's a good <u>friend</u>? Some people say that a real friend is someone who tells you <u>everything</u> about himself or herself, someone to whom you tell everything about <u>yourself</u>. Others disagree, and say that some things are <u>private</u>, and that it's not always important to share <u>everything</u> with friends—even good friends.

What do <u>you</u> think? Is a good friend someone who supports you no matter what, or is a good friend someone who tells you the truth, no matter what? Should a friend be similar to you—dress the way you dress, like the same things you like—or is it possible to have a good friend who's very <u>unlike</u> you?

What is <u>your</u> idea of what this "friendship thing" is all about?

Write about it, and give some examples.

### 3. (Betrayal)

Have you ever been betrayed by a friend, in a large or small way?

Being betrayed by a friend can be a shocking thing, whether that betrayal was in love ("She stole my boyfriend!") or situations less passionate ("You told the teacher!").

What happened? What did the betrayal feel like? Did it change your relationship, or did neither of you mention it, and life just went on? Or did talking about it—confronting your friend in his or her betrayal—make your relationship better?

And what about you: have <u>you</u> ever betrayed a friend, knowingly or unknowingly?

Write about it.

## 4. (Hurt Feelings—Intentional or Not)

Have you ever hurt someone's feelings deeply? Maybe that person was an adult, maybe a friend, maybe a relative.

Was your hurt intentional—on purpose—or was it done accidentally, almost unconsciously? Did the hurt come from words you said, or something you did? Did the person you hurt know right away, or find out later?

How did you know the person's feelings were hurt? And did you do anything to make the situation better? (Maybe you were <u>glad</u> their feelings were hurt?)

Finally, what did <u>they</u> do in response? Cry? Get angry? Become cold to you forever? Write about it.

## 5. (Crushes)

Everyone gets crushes: adults and kids alike. You see someone from across a crowded room and you're attracted to him or her, or you go to school with someone every day and like the way they walk and talk and twirl a pencil in their hands a certain way—it's all part of being human. Even very young kids get crushes.

Have you ever had a crush on someone who didn't know it? How long did you have that crush? What was it that made you like him or her so much? Did you ever tell anyone, or was it your special secret? Did that person ever find out? If so, how? If not, do you wish he or she did? Was life a little better—a little livelier—during the time you had your crush? Or worse?

Write about it.

## 6. (Making Friends)

Some people—good people—find it really difficult to make friends. They have trouble with knowing when to talk with someone, and <u>what to say</u> when they do finally talk with someone. For them, making friends can seem like a very complicated process—a mountain difficult to climb.

In your life, have <u>you</u> had a tough time making friends? If so, what has been hard about it? Did you ever succeed in making a friend, either lately or when you were a small child? What finally made you two friends?

Are there tricks to making friends—strategies people use to get closer to someone? What are they? Are there strategies you might try in the future?

Finally, if you're a person for whom it's <u>easy</u> to make friends, what are your secrets—how do you go about it?

### 7. (Friends, in Number)

Is it important to have a lot of friends? Does the number of friends you have mean much to you?

What do you think: is it better to have, say, ten friends who you consider "kind of" friends, or one friend you consider a <u>good</u> friend?

Have you known some people who seem to have a hundred friends, and others who have few? Do you think that kids with many friends are happier than those with few?

Why do you think some kids accumulate a lot of friends? What makes them do it? And why do you think some kids focus on just one or two friends? Do you think they'd like to be like those kids who have many friends, or do they think differently about what a <u>friend</u> is?

Why do you think the way you do about friends?

Write about it.

### 8. (Ulterior Motives)

Have you ever heard of an "ulterior motive"? A person has an <u>ulterior motive</u> when he or she pretends or says one thing, but really has <u>another</u> thing in mind.

Are you a person who has ulterior motives in dealing with friends? For instance, might you say something like, "Let's walk to the store—I haven't seen you for a while and it would be good to talk," when you really want information about a certain boy or girl?

Do you think kids have lots of ulterior motives in their relationships? Can you think of any examples of either you or your friends having ulterior motives?

And what about adults? Do you think adults sometimes pretend one thing, when what they really want is something entirely different—but they just don't say it?

Write about these things.

### 9. (Lending and Borrowing)

A character named Polonius in Shakespeare's <u>Hamlet</u> said, "Neither a borrower nor a lender be."

That seems pretty goofy, doesn't it? If no one lent anyone <u>anything</u> the world would be a pretty cold place.

But what <u>about</u> lending and borrowing? Have you had experience in lending things to friends, or to kids who weren't your friends? If so, how have those experiences been: did you get back what you lent, or did it disappear? If you didn't get it back right away, how did you manage to get it back?

And borrowing: are you "a borrower"? What do you borrow? Are you good about returning things on time, or do you delay? Has delay ever caused a problem?

Finally, if you were named the God of Lending and Borrowing, what would your rules be?

## 10. (Friends of Opposite Sex)

Do you have friends of the opposite sex, or do you confine yourself to friends of your same gender?

Some kids have known each other since early elementary school and have stayed close friends, their gender having little to do with their relationship. Others tend to stay away from the opposite sex, whether out of shyness or out of fear.

Does having friends of the opposite sex always mean that there is a romantic relationship involved, or is it possible for kids to have other-gender friends who are (really) "just friends"? If a kid would like to make friends with someone of the opposite sex, what advice would you give them? (Or give yourself?)

Finally, do you think that there is something extra to be gained—maybe in ways you might not have thought about before—in having a friend who's not of your gender?

Write about it.

## 11. (Long Overdue Letter)

You've been waiting for a long time, and today's the day to write that letter.

Write a letter to someone you've been meaning to write, but haven't had the chance to. Yes, e-mail is a form of letter writing, but it's not always as permanent as a letter written in someone's hand: someone whom the recipient (person who gets the letter) imagines putting pen to paper, pausing to think, putting pen to paper again.

To whom will you write? You decide. It might be a friend, a classmate, a relative who lives far away, or someone in your own house—someone to whom you'll take this letter today and deliver it personally.

Remember to date your letter, for it may be kept for a long time.

## 12. (Dislikes: People)

Not everyone likes everyone, but somehow, most days, most people get along.

Have you ever intensely disliked someone, or had someone intensely dislike you?

What were (are? no names, please) the reasons for the detestation (huge dislike)? A comment he or she made once, embarrassing you, or something different—envy, maybe, or an attitude on their part, or a certain behavior?

Maybe you received someone's dislike. What do you think you did to "deserve" it?

Finally, how did things resolve: did the anger melt away over the months or years, or do you (they?) still hold it? If it's still held, what do you think can be done to get rid of it?

Write about it.

### 13. (Change: Personal Development)

Often kids write in yearbooks, "Never change!"

Of course, we know they're not urging their friends never to change clothes, but what do they really mean?

What would it be like if kids your age never changed? What would they be like physically (their bodies), emotionally (their feelings), and intellectually (their minds)?

Are people meant not to change? What would the world be like if no one changed?

What is this about, this desire on people's part that their friends never change? Can your friends still be your friends if they change? Would you have to change with them, or could you accept their change? And do some people seem to stay the same all of their lives?

Write about it.

### 14. (Major Life-Changes)

Has there been a time when your life went through big changes? (Of course, this can be personal, and, as always, you needn't write about it.)

But everyone's life goes through major changes. Sometimes those changes are hard, sometimes exciting.

Perhaps you had to move, and needed to change schools, and left your friends behind. Or perhaps your family or social relationships changed, and you had to deal with it.

What was the change, and how did you deal with it? Was it difficult and stressful? Easy? Was it something you thought would be horrible, but it turned out well? Do you think you yourself changed as a result of a change that was forced on you?

Write about it.

### 15.  (Boys' Relationships with Boys, Girls' with Girls)

Do boys talk with each other the same way girls talk with each other?

Some say that boys don't actually talk too much to their friends—they use short sentences, not much description, talk about sports, and call each other names a lot.

Others say that girls have longer conversations, they are more gentle with each other ("tactful"), they say things more indirectly, and they gossip more.

Are these ideas just stereotypes? Is there really a difference at all between boys talking with boys and girls with girls, or are we all just humans talking with humans?

If you <u>do</u> think there's a difference, maybe write a little sample of dialogue as an example. If you <u>don't</u> think there's a difference, how do these stereotypes get started?

Write about it.

### 16.  (Differences Between Boys and Girls)

Do you think there are basic differences between boys and girls? OK—<u>ha, ha</u>—we <u>know</u> about the <u>physical</u> differences, but are there real, dividing <u>personality</u> differences?

There's a book called <u>Men Are from Mars, Women Are from Venus</u> (note the run-on sentence? ;-) ). In it the author claims that men and women have truly deep personality differences, and that it's not easy for the two genders to communicate.

What do you think? Do girls think a certain way and boys another way? <u>Act</u> a certain way? If that's true—and it may not be true—is a boy who acts "more like a girl" in your opinion less a <u>boy</u>, and a girl who "acts like a boy" less a <u>girl</u>? Or is the whole idea just a bunch of silly stereotypes?

Think about it, and write about it.

### 17.  (Relationship with Telephone)

What's your relationship with the telephone?

Some students hardly use the phone at all: either their parents forbid them, or their phone is always tied up by someone else in the house. Others have a phone in their pocket all the time, and seem constantly to be talking on the phone—even to the exclusion (cutting out) of talking with their friends who are right there next to them.

Who are you in this spectrum? Do you spend hours on the phone daily, or hardly any time? What would <u>your</u> life be like if there <u>were</u> no telephones, or if the entire telephone network collapsed for six months?

Write about it.

### 18.  (Arguments: Causes)

Everybody gets in arguments: kids, adults, people falling in love and out of love, <u>everybody</u>.

When kids argue at school, what are they mostly arguing about? Even in our school, you can hear kids getting into disagreements as they walk down the hall or hang out in the yard. Not <u>fights</u> but disagreements. It's normal, but it's interesting to try to figure out what such arguments are about.

Do <u>things</u> (material objects and possessions) figure into many arguments? For example, one kid having more cool games than another, or more money than another? Or are <u>people</u> mostly the issue: boyfriend/girlfriend conflicts, jealousy/envy issues, etc.

In your own experience, what do <u>you</u> mostly get into verbal conflicts about? Write about it.

### 19.  (Strategies for Avoiding Conflicts)

What are some good strategies for solving conflicts, both among your friends and among other kids?

Everyone experiences conflicts—arguments small and large. But not everyone has strategies to solve them, and problems can grow much worse if things aren't remediated.

What have you done in <u>your</u> life to "make things better" in arguments or disagreements, either with friends or with parents? Is there a cool way to make things smooth again, or is every situation different?

And what about among friends or brothers or sisters—do you sometimes observe a problem and help the others communicate and come to understanding? What are your tricks—or, if you haven't used your own skills, what have you noticed other kids do?

Write about it.

### 20.  (Advice to Adults: How to Communicate with Kids)

If you could give advice to adults, what ways would you suggest for them to improve their communication with kids?

Clearly, the way some adults communicate with kids offends kids and makes them angry. What do adults do that is so far off base in talking with kids? What do they say and do that results in situations' being made worse instead of better?

If you were to write a letter to "Mr. Adult," or "Ms. Adult," what would you say that would result in better feelings between kids and adults?

Adults, like kids, often need examples, so try to give some.

### 21. (Kids' Version of House Rules)

If you were an adult and you had kids your age, what would the rules of your house be?

What responsibilities around the house would your kids have and not have? How much would your kids be responsible for shopping, cooking, cleaning, and taking care of little brothers and sisters? Would they have more responsibility than you, or less?

Would you give your kids an allowance? If so, how much? (Really: no exaggeration here.) If not, why?

Would your kids have to be home by a certain time? If so, what time? If not, why?

What about grades? Would your kids have to achieve certain grades or get in trouble?

And what if your child got in trouble at school? How would you handle it?

Write about it.

### 22. (Switch Roles Day)

Let's pretend that next Tuesday was designated "National Parent-Child/Teacher-Child Switch Day." On that day, it would be mandatory for parents and children and teachers and children to switch places: the kids in charge, the parents and teachers having to do what the kids say.

How would you handle the situation? Would you be the sweetest parent to your parent and the kindest teacher to your teachers? Would you mix sweet kindness with "a taste of their own medicine"? Or would you go to the other side entirely—exacting cruel revenge for past wrongs? (Remember: everything you do has to be legal! ;-) )

Write about it.

### 23. (Observing Adults with Adults)

What is it like for you, as a kid, to watch adults interacting with adults?

What do you learn about adults by watching them and listening to them when they're with each other?

Do you think they're honest, mostly, with each other? Do the adults you see model for you what you want to be like, act like, and talk like? Are there some examples you can cite of family members or teachers or friends being really <u>cool</u> and <u>respectful</u> and <u>kind</u> and <u>helpful</u> with each other? (Alas, are there other examples of the opposite—examples, perhaps, of dishonesty or disrespect or hypocrisy?)

Write about it.

## 24.   (Arguments vs. Discourse)

The ancient Greeks used to stand in public areas in the middle of cities and argue about things all day—just for fun. Then they'd shake hands and go home. Next day, same thing.

When people argue, do you think it means they don't like each other? Let's say one person loves the President and the other person despises him. Does that mean they're enemies?

Maybe you think so. If so, why does that have to be the case? How can we talk about things as a people if that is the case? Maybe you think not. If not, why does it seem that when people argue about things like politics and religion they get so mad at each other, they often go away steaming?

Should there be any rules about arguing with people—rules that we all understand and go by? If so, what should those rules be? If not, how can we stop our anger over differing ideas from becoming much worse, and escalating into wars?

Write about it.

## 25.   (Bullies)

Have you ever been bothered by a bully?

Some bullies push younger kids around in elementary school. But we all know that bullies exist in both middle school and high school.

If you've been bullied, what were your experiences with that bully? Did he or she want money? Did you get hurt? Did the bully prey upon you, hassling you often? Did you tell anyone? Did anyone help? Did you finally stand up to the bully, or avoid him or her? Was the bully ever caught, or did he or she continue his or her bullying?

And what about the opposite—have <u>you</u> ever bullied anyone? What did you do? How did you feel? What do you think when you look back on it now?

Write about it.

## SORTING OUT THE WORLD

### 26. (Changing the Way Things Run)

When it comes to the way our government is run—and what the world will be like when you grow up—what do you worry about?

Some students worry deeply about our schools: how good they are or will be, how much funding they get, and how strong an education they'll finally offer.

Other students worry about other things: poverty (themselves and others), homelessness, violence and what is done or not done about it, prisons, public transportation—a whole range of concerns.

Where are you in this spectrum? What do you think about how the world is now and how it might be? Is there one big issue that worries you, or do many things in our society worry you?

Write about it.

### 27. (Distribution of Wealth)

Clearly, some people have more money than others. Some have a lot more money than others.

Do you think it's fair that in our society some people are very rich and some are very poor?

The rich man might say, "Hey! I worked for my money twelve hours a day for forty years! I earned it! Those poor people sit around all day watching TV!"

The poor man might say, "Hey! If I could get a job, I would, but there are no jobs out there! That rich guy has sent all his company's jobs overseas!"

What's fair, in your opinion? Should such a distance between rich and poor exist in our country? If so, why? If not, what system would you devise to change things?

Write about it.

### 28. (Solutions for Homelessness)

What would you do about the homelessness situation in our country? Certainly, most people do not choose to be homeless: they'd like to have an apartment or a house to go home to, a roof over their heads, and a steady income.

How do you think people become homeless in the first place? Can there be a number of reasons? Do you think there are people who actually want to be homeless?

And what can be done to help solve homelessness? What ideas do <u>you</u> have to make things better for homeless men, women, and children? (How will your program be paid for?)

Write about it.

### 29. (Borders: Aliens)

As if they had dropped from outer space, someone who enters our country illegally is called an <u>illegal alien.</u> What they did was cross a <u>border</u>—a line in the sand, so to speak. When they crossed that line, they were in another country altogether.

Do you think borders should exist? What is it that makes one place "Mexico," say, and another place, just a few feet away, "The United States of America"?

Are borders between countries useful? What purpose do they serve?

What would it be like in our world if borders were dissolved and there were no lines between countries anymore? What would it be like if there were no <u>countries</u> anymore?

Think about it, and write about it.

### 30. (Causes of Wars: Seeds)

As you know, there's always a war going on <u>somewhere</u> in the world.

What causes wars, in your opinion? How do people in a whole country get so mad at another whole country that they decide to bomb buildings and kill young people and old people, men, women, and children?

Are wars about land? Oil? Hurt feelings? Racism? What do you think?

Finally, do you think that <u>going to war</u> has any relation to people's abilities to solve personal problems and arguments? Can little wars start at home, in the way we treat each other, and escalate to big wars against other people?

Write about it.

### 31. (What Is Wild?)

The word <u>wild</u> has so many meanings. It can mean <u>primitive</u> or <u>uncontrolled</u> or <u>reckless</u> or <u>uncivilized.</u> The word itself can trigger many connotations (other meanings that "jump up" out of words) inside us.

What is <u>the wild</u> for you? Some people consider the wild to be animals in deep, remote (far away) forests, but others think of cityscapes as well: the wild things that go on in cities. Still others think of profound silence (that found in the desert, for example) as wild. The wild, some say, can even be found inside of us if we look deeply enough.

Do a little written meditation on the word <u>wild</u>. Name the things that come to mind when you think of the word, and try to describe those things in detail.

### 32.   (Noise Pollution)

There are many kinds of pollution: pollution of the air, water, and land.

But what about what's called <u>noise pollution</u>? Does it bother you, and should something be done about it?

Noise pollution is a little hard to define. Really, it's noise that bothers people: "gets on their nerves." It's something that's too loud for either a long or short time.

Are there noises in the world that bother you? (Some people might be offended by loud radios, while those carrying the loud radios might think <u>motorcycles</u> or <u>jack hammers</u> are too loud.)

What "sets your alarm off" when it comes to noise pollution?

Finally, if you could make rules about noise pollution in our world, what rules would you put into place?

Write about it.

### 33.   (Pollution, Witnessed)

People say they want our world to be <u>clean</u>, but often don't do much about it.

What kinds of pollution do you notice? Of course, there's air pollution, water pollution, land pollution (litter, toxic waste, etc.), and noise pollution.

Have you witnessed people polluting in any of these categories? What have you noticed people do to make the air dirtier? The water? The land?

Write about what you've seen, both on the part of adults and on the part of kids. Write about what you'd do about it if you had the power.

### 34.   (What to Ban in the World?)

If you ruled the world for a day, what would you outlaw, or ban?

Would you ban huge things, like war, or smaller things, like noisy barking dogs? Would you outlaw certain behaviors, like spitting in the street, or using clichés, or getting divorced, or wearing skirts? Would you outlaw certain "isms," like racism or ageism?

Brainstorm with yourself a little, and write as many things as you can—large and small—that you'd ban, and tell <u>why</u> you'd ban them.

## 35. (Discarded Items)

Do you ever notice things being thrown away that still could be used by someone?

Sometimes <u>food</u> is thrown away when it's still good. Other times it's clothing, appliances, items of furniture—even, sometimes, whole interiors of houses. Some people say we're a <u>consumer</u> society: we buy things, then, when the newest model comes along, throw the old one away.

What have <u>you</u> noticed about things being discarded in our society? What have you seen thrown away? Do you think that there are people who could <u>use</u> those things? If so, what sort of system could you devise (figure out) to <u>get</u> these discarded things to people?

Finally, do you think this "use it/discard it" attitude exists in all countries? Have you ever been in a country where it's different?

Write about it.

## 36. (Solve One World Problem)

Of course, along with all the joys of living in our world, we've got our problems.

If you could solve <u>one</u> of the world's problems, which one would you choose? One student might choose the problem of poverty. Others might attack war, or homelessness, pollution, global warming, child abuse, or any other of the myriad maladies we hear about every day.

What would be <u>your</u> project, and how would you go about solving it? What ideas do you have to make things better in the problem area you choose?

Write about it.

## 37. (What Does Crazy Mean?)

Anyone who has spent any time in school or out in the streets has heard someone say, "You're crazy!"

Crazy to think about it, maybe, but what <u>is</u> crazy? Are there different kinds of crazy?

Have <u>you</u> ever known anyone <u>you</u> thought was crazy? If so, what exactly do you mean by <u>crazy</u>? What are some examples of things they said or did to make you think that? Were they a danger to anyone else, or, perhaps, a danger to themselves?

And is there <u>another</u> kind of crazy—a creative, <u>alive</u> crazy that describes someone whom people enjoy being around? What is <u>that</u> crazy about, and why do people act that way?

Finally, what would the world be like without crazy people? Would it be as interesting? Would you prefer it?

Write about these things.

### 38. (Devise Punishment/Prison System)

If people do things that society says are "wrong," should they be punished?

Let's assume you think they <u>should</u> be punished. If you think so, then how should people be punished? Should a murderer be murdered and a thief have all of his or her things taken away?

Should there be prisons? If so, how much time should people spend in prisons for various crimes? Do you believe that if someone commits a certain number of crimes he or she should spend an entire lifetime in prison? Could people be allowed <u>out</u> of prisons early sometimes—before their sentence is up? In what circumstances?

What would prisons be like, in your world of justice?

Write about it.

### 39. (Ownership of Land)

People own houses. Those houses sit on land. Other people own <u>plenty</u> of land—sometimes miles of it. Landowners have a piece of paper called a <u>deed</u> that says they own their land.

Do you think it's really possible for people to own land? That is to say, "These rocks and these trees and this part of this river belongs to Josephine Jones."

The earth is five billion years old. People, obviously, lead much shorter lives.

Do you think it's fair that people "own" land? Is owning land a solid idea, or a goofy idea?

What would the world be like if people couldn't "own" land? How would things change?

Write about it.

### 40. (Fences: Functions)

There's an old Robert Frost poem in which a man says, "Good fences make good neighbors."

What do you think that means, "Good fences make good neighbors."

Do you agree with it? Do you think that a fence between people—a boundary—makes people get along better?

What would the world be like if there were no fences—if all of a sudden a law was passed mandating people to tear down all fences: how would the world change? What would the world look like? Do you think people's behavior might change?

Write about it.

(Of course, if you want to write about emotional fences, that's great, too.)

### 41. (Witnessed Something You Wish You Hadn't)

Have you ever witnessed something that you wish you hadn't seen?

Such a "something" can have many possibilities: it could have been an auto accident, a young child being slapped brutally by his mother in a supermarket, or something that happened at someone's house when you were visiting—something you wish you hadn't been there for.

Whatever it was, you wish you could push the "rewind" button and erase it, but now you can't.

Write about it, in as much detail as you want.

### 42. (Family Member Elected to Office)

If you could elect one member of your family to a public office—say, President, or Governor, or Member of Congress—whom would you elect?

Some students of course might choose to elect no one in their family, but others might particularly admire a grandparent, mom, dad, uncle, aunt, or even brother or sister.

To which office (President, Governor, Mayor, etc.) would you elect that person?

Why do you choose that relative, and what kinds of things do you imagine him or her doing once he or she were in office? How would this person help change the world?

(Maybe you'll choose yourself as that "relative"!)

Write about it.

### 43. (Personal Privacy: Important?)

How important is personal privacy to you? Do you get enough privacy in your life?

For some people, lots of privacy is very important. They want their own room, lots of time uninterrupted by other people, and their secrets known by no one.

Others, though, don't care much about privacy. They look on their world as a public space, one to which everyone is invited, all day, all the time.

What strategies do you use to get your privacy, if privacy is important to you? What frustrates you at home or at school in your desire for privacy?

If privacy is <u>not</u> important to you, why do you think it's not so important—what are your beliefs or your attitudes that make privacy no big deal?

Write about it.

## 44. (Best Way to Teach History?)

Some people love studying history. Some hate it.

If you were a teacher and you had the opportunity to devise a <u>really good</u> way to study history, what system would you come up with?

Would you use books? Videos? Slides?

What kinds of activities would you do? Would kids read from books and do the questions at the end of the chapter? How much discussion would you have? How much group activity? How would you know if kids were "getting it"—that is, how would you "test" them on their knowledge?

Write about it.

## 45. (Visit a Historical Time)

What historical time do you wish you could visit?

Of course, <u>the future</u> is not historical yet, but think about particular times in the past. Maybe you'd like to visit ancient Egypt and live there for a while. Maybe you'd like to have been an Inca in South America, or a Roman soldier fighting Carthage, or a writer during the Italian Renaissance.

Maybe you'd only like to go back a <u>short</u> distance—say, to the 1960s, to visit the hippie days in San Francisco.

Write about the time you'd like to visit, <u>why</u> you'd like to visit that time, and what you'd do while you were there.

## 46. (Design a Curriculum)

If you could design a curriculum for kids your age—that is, the classes they would take in school—what would you design? <u>Seriously?</u>

Would you schedule the usual classes—English, math, science, etc., or would you add <u>other</u> classes that you think are important—or, if not important, classes that would be cool or useful?

How would you make sure that the basic skills were taught? What specifically would you do to make sure that kids learned to read, write, and do math and science in a smart and sophisticated way?

What would your day-to-day schedule be? What electives would you add? Would students stay in the school building all day long, or go out, either occasionally or for extended periods of time?

What about homework? Would there be more? Less? What would the homework be?

Write about it.

## 47.    (Too Much Homework?)

Some students, apparently, are complaining that there's too much homework and that they're staying up until midnight completing what's assigned.

What's <u>your</u> opinion? Do you think you have too much homework? On <u>average</u> how many hours (minutes? ;-) ) do you spend doing homework per night? Do you usually have homework on weekends? If so, how much?

Of course, kids have been complaining about homework since the days of the ancient Greeks (ancient Geeks? ;-) ), but have you noticed a recent change in the amount of homework required?

Finally, two things: do you sometimes <u>learn</u> from homework? <u>And</u>, are you one of those students who leaves the big stuff—reports and projects—until the very last minute?

Write about these things.

## 48.    (Prediction of Future World)

What does the future hold for us? If you could project us a hundred years into the future, what kind of world would we be living in?

What do you think our transportation system will be like? Our school system? How will we be communicating? Will human relationships be the same? What will the health system be like? Will people be pursuing happiness, as our Declaration of Independence claims we have a right to do, or will we be slaves of government or corporations?

Write about it.

## 49. (Gun Problems)

The United States has more gun-related deaths and injuries than any industrialized country. Citizens of most countries are not even allowed to own guns—possession of one is a serious crime. In countries that <u>do</u> allow gun ownership, citizens must <u>register</u> them so that if a crime is committed, police can track down the gun's owner.

Few people here, though, know who has guns and who doesn't. Some people say <u>good</u>: after all, our Constitution guarantees "the right to bear arms." Others say that we're a country of fools—we don't seem to care if our citizens—crazy or sane—keep guns and shoot each other in anger.

Do you support our national policy—or our <u>lack</u> of national policy—on guns? If so, why? Do you think that gun violence should be controlled? What, then, should be done to control guns and to stop the violence? And what do we do with the 300,000,000 guns said to exist in people's homes?

Write about it.

## 50. (Noticing Drivers' Behavior)

Anyone wandering around our world for a while has an opportunity to observe many different kinds of drivers.

What do you notice about people who drive cars? Are there real differences between drivers? If they're different, what are those differences? Have you seen people do crazy or dangerous things while driving? Have you seen people do kind things? Do you think that the way people drive reflects their personalities? (Do you think some people's personalities <u>change</u> when they get behind the wheel?)

(Let's hope not, but have you ever been involved in an accident?)

Finally, what kind of driver do <u>you</u> want to be? What models do you want to follow?

Write about it.

## 51. (Enough Vacation Time in U.S.?)

Do you think people in our country get enough vacation time? How much time do your parents and relatives take off to spend with their families, get a few things done around the house, or just relax?

Many countries in the world mandate four to six weeks' paid vacation for every worker every year. Here in the United States, the situation is more often around two weeks' vacation. That's a big difference, psychologists say.

Is vacation from work or school important? How much vacation do you think people should have, both from work and from school?

Do you think that if your family members had more vacation your life would change? If so, in what ways?

Write about it.

### 52. (Boys'/Girls' Treatment in School)

Do you think there's a difference in the way boys and girls are treated in school?

Do teachers, for example, tend to call more on girls than on boys, or is it the opposite? Are girls given the same opportunities as boys, and vice versa? What about in physical education: do you think that girls and boys have the same opportunities? And then, of course, there's <u>behavior</u>. Who gets into trouble more—boys or girls? Does that group <u>deserve</u> to get into trouble more? How do things in school generally even out—or do they?

Write about it.

### 53. (Undeserved Trouble)

Have you ever gotten into trouble—either at home or at school—for something about which you were completely innocent? If so, what happened, how did you try to convince the adult that you were innocent, and what were the consequences? What were your feelings at the time?

In general, do you think that kids are accused of things more readily (blamed for things) than adults? Do you think that either at home or out in the "big world" kids are suspected of things more than adults? Are there any grounds (reasons) for those suspicions? Do kids <u>deserve</u> those suspicions?

Write about it.

### 54. (Rudeness Defined)

Perhaps different people have different conceptions of what <u>rudeness</u> is. What is <u>your</u> idea of rudeness? Is the guy on the crowded bus who sits in the aisle seat and puts his little grocery bag on the seat beside him so that no one will sit there <u>rude</u>? Is the woman who spits on the street <u>rude</u>? Is the friend (or <u>teacher</u>?) who passes you in the empty hall and doesn't greet you <u>rude</u>? What is rudeness, after all?

Give examples of rudeness that you've witnessed in your life, whether this school year or in the past. (Also, although I'm sure it's very unlikely, have there ever been times when you yourself have been rude—perhaps made some faux pas or blunder—and lived to regret it?)

Write about it.

### 55. (Clichés)

Many people complain that in our spoken life, certain words are used so often they lose meaning.

We hear the word "cute" a lot, for example. We hear people say, "He has cute eyes," or "That blouse is cute."

Is "cute" a word that is overused? Can you think of other words in our world that are overused? If so, which words are they, and do you use those words very often?

Finally, is there a danger to our language when we overuse words so much that they become clichés and lose their meaning? Does calling something "cute," for example, really insult the thing itself by making it something a lot less complicated (and beautiful) than it is? Are we lazy users of language when we use these words?

What do you think? Write about it.

### 56. (U.S. as World Leader)

How is the United States doing as the world's leader?

Clearly, we are the world's leader: we have the biggest military, a huge economy, and a great influence on what happens in the world.

Are we using our leadership well? Are we working as a force for good things to happen to the peoples of the world, or are we doing the opposite? Are we successful in some places and a failure in others? What examples can you give to show how we're doing well or badly?

Finally, what should we be doing in the world, as its most powerful nation?

Write about it.

### 57. ("State of Union")

Every year the President of the United States gives a speech called the "State of the Union Address." In it he (or she, one day?) talks to the Congress about how things are going in our country.

Today, put down some thoughts for your own State of the Union Address, if you were to make the same speech.

How are things going in our country? Are you satisfied with everything? What is working in our country, and what is not working? Think about schools, transportation, national defense, our system of health care, the arts, protection of the environment, food stamps, welfare, treatment of the elderly, and other things that make up <u>who we are</u> as a people.

Be the President for a day, and tell us how we're doing as a country.

### 58. (Importance of Money)

How important is money in the world?

Some people say that money is everything: if you don't have it, you're miserable, and your family is miserable. Other people say that money means nothing: that it's what's <u>inside</u> a person that counts, and happiness or misery depend on who you are as a person and how you live your life. Still others say that money's place is somewhere in the middle: somewhat important, but not all-important.

What is the role of money in <u>your</u> life? Is it something you think about all the time, wish you had more of, and scheme in your daydreams ways to get? Or is money of secondary importance—something you think you have enough of, something to get you your basic needs, having little to do with happiness?

Write about it.

### 59. (Relative Importance of Jobs)

Is one person's job more important than another person's job?

Is a doctor's job more important than a teacher's? Is a teacher's more important than a bus driver's? Is a dishwasher's job more important than a lawyer's? Is a business executive's job more important than that of a woman who sews dresses?

How do you determine how important a job is? Obviously, some people take home bigger salaries than others: is <u>that</u> how job importance is rated?

Write about it.

## GOOFY AND IMAGINATIVE

### 60. (Sudden Ability to Fly)

What if you woke up one morning, got out of bed, and discovered you could fly? What would you do that day?

Would you tell anyone of your new powers, or keep them a secret? Would you go to school that day, or play "aerial hooky"?

How would you structure your flying day: would you fly around school, down the halls and into the schoolyard, or would you plan something wider: maybe world-wider?

What would you see? What would you do? Would you have an organized itinerary (travel plan), minute by minute and hour by hour, or would you let your whim and the wind take you?

Write about it.

### 61.    (Sudden Invisibility)

In a dream a voice comes to you: "My friend, when you wake up you will have the power, for one day only, to be invisible. Simply say the word 'kazaam,' and you'll be so. Say 'kazoom,' and you'll be back."

Strange dream, you think, but when you wake up you find it's true. You say the words, and they work!

What would you do that day? You have twenty-four hours to move through the world either completely invisible, invisible sometimes, or visible all the time, as we are.

Would you stay around your family and friends? Would you travel through the countryside or through the city? Would you play tricks, using your voice sometimes?

Think about it. Write about it.

### 62.    (Power to See Underwater)

What if you had the power, suddenly and for a period of one month, not only to breathe under water, but to see perfectly under water? Would you use this power, or simply ignore it and live your life the way you've always lived it?

If you used your power, what would you do? Find every swimming pool you could and swim around? Go to a lake you know and see what's inside it? Find the nearest ocean and explore? (If so, what would you explore, and why?)

Would you perhaps use your power to help people in some way?

Write about it.

### 63.    (Choose or Create Own Superhero)

If you could choose to be any superhero you'd like, which one would you choose? Would you be Superman, able to bend steel in his bare hands and leap tall buildings in a single bound? Would you be Wonder Woman, saving the world from nefarious villains, or Spider Man, climbing skyscrapers toward heroic action?

Or would you create your <u>own</u> superhero and become her or him—Laser Girl, for example, or Fuel-Injected Boy, able to—? (Would you have disguises? A uniform? Special weaknesses? A sidekick?)

Finally, since we all know that superheroes are the world's great problem-solvers, what problems would you choose to tackle?

Write about it.

### 64. (Healing Touch)

Stories go far back in literature about people with a <u>healing touch</u>: people with the ability simply to touch a person, and that "touched" person is healed of whatever affliction he or she has.

What if <u>you</u> had the "healing touch" for a short period of time—say, a week? And what if, given that "gift," no one was able to know that it was <u>you</u> who healed them through your touch?

What would you do? Go around touching everyone and healing everyone of their ailments? Or would you start with particular people: say, family members or friends, and cure them of their maladies? How would you plan your week?

Think about it, then write about it.

### 65. (One Super Power)

The motif of <u>Superman</u> has always been attractive to people: a guy who can fly, is super-strong, and has X-ray vision.

What if for one day you had only <u>one</u> of these abilities: that of super strength? What would you do with it? Would you show off a little to your family and friends? Would you change the shape of things that have always bothered you? Destroy something? Build something? Would you help people in some way? (Remember: you can't fly—only have super strength!)

Think about it, then write about it.

### 66. (Unlimited Travel)

If someone gave you a plane ticket for anywhere in the world and unlimited money for three months, what would you do? The rules: you <u>may</u> visit many places—not just one—and the money must be used for living expenses in the places to which you fly (food, hotel, entertainment, maybe a few souvenirs).

Where would you go? Would you stay in this country, or visit others? Which others, and why? What sights would you like to see in those places? Would you stay in fancy hotels, or clean, inexpensive ones? Would you try new foods? (If so, what new foods?)

Write about it.

### 67. (Sudden Superstar)

If you could suddenly be a superstar, what sort of superstar would you be?

Some students might choose to become the best ballet dancer in the history of the art. Others might choose to be the best baseball player, or the most popular movie star, or the greatest singer <u>ever</u>.

What would be your chosen "genre" (field) of superstardom, and what would you do every day? How would you use your wealth and fame?

Write about it.

### 68. (Celebrity Falls in Love with You)

An airy fairy appears to you one day and says, "My friend, you are the chosen one. For one day, the movie star or music star you choose will fall in love with you. The only catch is that you have to justify your choice in writing."

If that crazy thing were to happen, whom would you choose? Would it be someone famous, or not-so-well-known? Are you familiar with their work—their films or their music? Is it their work that attracts you, or their personality, or the way they look? What would you <u>write</u> to justify (make a good case for) your choice, and therefore get this dreamy date?

Write it!

### 69. (Spend $200)

What if someone walked into the classroom and gave you not a trillion or a billion or a million dollars, but <u>two</u> <u>hundred</u> dollars?

It's easy enough to wildly write about what you'd do with a million dollars, but you know what things <u>really</u> cost, and it's a real challenge to plan for how to spend two hundred dollars.

Would you go to the bank and get five-dollar bills and pass them out to the class, saving fifty bucks for your wonderful teacher? ;-) Would you throw a huge pizza party for the class?

Or would you be more thoughtful: buy something you've always wanted, or help out your family somehow. (Maybe you'd do a <u>combination</u> of things.)

Write about it, and tell why you'd do the things you'd do.

## 70.  (Solve Two Problems)

If you were suddenly given the power to solve <u>two</u> problems, and only two problems, which would you solve?

Some students might choose worldwide problems: world hunger, for example, or the horror of AIDS. Others might choose problems at school or at home: problems directly involving them.

Describe the problems you are solving, so we can get a good idea of the issues you're writing about, and be sure to tell <u>why</u> you'd choose these particular problems to solve over all the others.

## 71.  (Everyone Imitates You)

If a day came along when you had the power to force everyone in the world to eat the food you love, like the things you like, and do the things you like to do, what would you force people to do?

For example, would the whole world be eating rocky road ice cream that day, then going to the dance club at school? Would the whole world fall in love with one song from a certain CD? Would the whole world fall in love with one boy or girl? Play basketball all day long?

Write about it, and take the world through your favorites.

## 72.  (Love Potion)

<u>Love potions</u> are an old theme in stories. Shakespeare's <u>A Midsummer Night's Dream</u> features a love potion that, when drunk, causes the drinker to fall in love with the first person (or animal!) he or she sees.

If <u>you</u> could concoct a "love potion," to whom (to what?) would you administer it? Would there be a few people in your own life to whom you'd like to give a love potion, or do you prefer to let your imagination go wild and think of some goofy pairings: one famous politician with another, one particular superstar with a walrus . . . who knows?

What would you do with your own, specially brewed, love potion?

Write about it.

## 73.  (Trickster)

As you know, the <u>trickster</u> is present in many American Indian stories. Sometimes the trickster takes the form of a <u>coyote</u>, sometimes not.

If you could spend a day having the power to play tricks on people, what tricks would you play, and on whom?

Would you choose family members to trick? Famous people? Friends? Classmates? (Horror of horrors, <u>teachers</u>?)

What kinds of tricks would you do? Just one, over and over, or a whole bag of tricks?

Write about it.

## THE NATURAL WORLD

### 74. (Rainy Days)

It's raining today. A strange thing: the sky darkens, a heavy feeling hangs in the air, and water starts falling from the sky.

Do you like the rain? Do you find it inconvenient, as some people claim, or does it give you other feelings? Can rain be exciting? Can it evoke (bring out) other feelings in you? Is the rain mysterious to you? Do you have memories of certain rainy days in your childhood, and what you did (or didn't do?) on those days?

Write about the rain today.

### 75. (Windy Days)

Teachers swear that windy days are difficult: that kids are more excited than usual, and hard to calm down.

Do you agree that wind can be exciting? A big gust hitting you as you come around a corner, or a steady blast of wind across the schoolyard? What's so exciting about wind?

And where do you think wind comes from, anyway? How is it made? Do you think it travels far, or begins nearby? Are you a "fan" of wind ;-), or do you dislike it?

Write about these things.

### 76. (Rodent Attitude)

What are your thoughts and feelings about snakes and rodents (rats, mice, etc.)?

Some people are crazy about them; they study them, keep them in cages or aquariums—even breed them.

Other people abhor them—can't stand them. They wouldn't enter a building in which they knew a snake—even a nonpoisonous snake—was loose. Others despise rats and mice, even to the point of having bad dreams about them.

What about you? Do you have strong feelings about snakes or rodents? Do you know much about snakes and rodents? Have you had personal experience with either or both of them?

Write about it, and think about using your descriptive powers in this entry.

## 77.   (Insect Attitude)

How do you feel about insects? Do they "bug" you, or are you interested in them?

Some people can't stand to touch "bugs," and are afraid when they see a bee or a sow bug.

Others are fascinated by insects: the thousands of types of colorful butterflies, strange-looking praying mantises, even spiders and flies.

What's <u>your</u> relationship with insects—those millions of critters living with us in our everyday world? Why do you think you feel the way you feel? Have you had particular incidents or experiences with insects that make you feel the way you do?

Write about it.

## 78.   (Attention to Birds)

Do you pay much attention to birds? In the city, of course, there are pigeons aplenty, but also often (depending on where people live) sea gulls, blackbirds, sparrows, crows, ravens, mockingbirds—even hawks. Kids who live in the country have many more bird species in their environment.

Have you ever really <u>observed</u> birds, and what they do? Looked and listened to them? Watched their patterns? If so, what have you noticed? Do you have favorite birds?

Finally, what would our world be like <u>without</u> birds?

Write about it.

## 79.   (Thinking about the Cosmos)

Do you ever look at the stars? Do you ever think about the universe?

Of course, what we see in the night sky is our own solar system and our own galaxy, the Milky Way. But there's so much more: the universe is almost larger than we can imagine, and includes what scientists call black holes, quasars, red dwarfs, and other cool-sounding things that describe celestial (heavenly) phenomena (extraordinary things).

What do you think about when you look at the stars or think about the stars and the universe? Is it all so big that it scares you? Do you think about us here, on this little earth, rolling through our days?

Write about what you know (or questions you have?) about the universe, and what you think when you think about it.

## 80. (Balance of Nature)

We hear people talking about the balance of nature. What is the balance of nature, in your opinion? We know that nature consists of air, water, land, flora (plants), fauna (animals), and insects.

How can those things be "in balance"? How do you think the natural system works, in its push toward keeping itself balanced?

Do you think the natural world is in balance today? If so, what keeps it in balance? If not, what's knocking it out of balance?

And what about human beings—people? Where are we in the balance of nature? What are we doing or not doing to keep our balance?

Write about it.

## 81. (Favorite Water Form)

When it comes to bodies of water, what form is your favorite? Are you a river person, a lake person, or an ocean person? Think about having to choose one of those and writing a defense (argument) in the river's voice, or the lake's, or the ocean's.

Tell us in that river-voice or lake-voice or ocean-voice what's so good about you: why should we choose you to spend time with or study or simply pay more attention to?

Write about your watery self.

## 82. (Underground Imaginings)

TV nature-shows often focus on amazing things under the sea or amazing things on the surface of the earth.

Have you ever thought of what's going on—as we write today, even—underground? Below the street or soil just a few inches, or a few feet, or half a mile, or whole miles?

There's so much going on: of the human world, the insect, the animal, even the water.

Pretend you have X-ray goggles on and can see <u>below</u> the surface of the earth. Focus a while in your mind's eye, and <u>see</u>. What do you see under there?

If you like, think about beginning each paragraph with "I see."

Tell us what's down there.

### 83. (Careful Observations)

Have you ever taken time—a few minutes or longer—and really <u>watched</u> something or someone? That <u>something</u> might be a spider making its web, a cat grooming herself, a pot of blue flowers visited by bees and butterflies, or many things. What in the natural world have you watched, and what did you notice?

On the human side, have you ever closely observed someone and noticed what they do: whether in class, on the street, or at home?

If you've done either (or both) of these things, describe what you saw. (Or see, now? ;-) )

### 84. (Build an Animal)

As you know, lots of animals have specialties—things they do <u>really</u> well. The gazelle is a graceful runner, the lion a terrific hunter, the giraffe skilled at eating leaves from <u>very</u> high trees. Certainly, nature is wonderful in plenty, but...

If <u>you</u> could build a really cool animal—invent one yourself out of important parts of existing animals—what would you come up with? A creature with a crocodile head with the legs of a gazelle, the body of a brown bear and a coral-snake tail? How would your animal function in the world? What would its daily life be like? What would you name it?

Write about the beast.

### 85. (Improve on Nature)

It seems that nature's done a pretty good job. The world is an elegant and beautiful and ordered place. But let's be bold.

Do you have any criticisms of the way nature works things? For instance, are there any problems with the design of (or what happens to) the human body? Would you make any changes in weather patterns, if you could? Are you happy with the way rivers flow, the way fish swim, the length of the lives of humans or animals or trees, the nature of death?

What would you change about the natural world if you had the power?

Write about it.

## TAKING RISKS; ASPIRATIONS

### 86. (Risks Taken)

What kind of <u>risks</u> have you taken in your life? What <u>chances</u> have you taken that may or may not have come out so well?

Some kids have tried some dangerous things and survived. (Many others, alas, have <u>not</u> survived.) Other kids have taken other kinds of risks: social risks such as trying to make new friends, for example, or personal risks, such as speaking honestly to a parent, or even academic risks: doing something in class that might get them a great grade or result in a horrible failure.

What risks have <u>you</u> taken in your life?

Write about them.

### 87. (Survival Strategies)

Have you ever thought about having to <u>survive</u> somewhere? Think about being dropped into a place: say, the middle of a strange city, a deep forest, a desert, a tropical island, or a snowy mountain, and having to survive there for a month.

Choose only <u>one</u> of those places—or, of course, a place <u>you</u> think of—and plan, in words, methods you'd use to survive. What would your shelter be? (Would you even need one?) How would you keep warm? How would you get food and water? Would you do <u>such</u> a good job that you'd even have room for luxuries, such as books to read, or fancy contraptions that would fan you in sizzling weather?

Think about your survival strategies, and write about them.

### 88. (What Sort of Adult to Be?)

Think about yourself as an adult. What kind of adult do you want to be?

Certainly, except for staying in shape and watching what we eat and drink, we can't do much about our <u>physical</u> selves: what we'll look like.

But what about your <u>inner</u> self? How will you act toward your husband, or wife, or domestic partner? How will you act toward your kids, if you have kids? (Will you spend much time with them?)

Will you be a peacemaker in your life, or a conflict-maker? How will you spend your free time? Will you cheat a little to get ahead in business? Will you want privacy? Will you have a <u>garden</u>? Will you <u>read</u>?

Write about your future self, and who you'll be.

### 89.  (Risks to Be Taken)

As you think about planning your life as the person you'll be in the future, what kinds of <u>risks</u> would you <u>like</u> to take?

Of course, <u>wanting</u> to do something and actually <u>doing</u> it are two different things, but today play around with just <u>thinking</u> about the future <u>you</u>.

What risks would you like to take in your social life? What risks would you like to take in thinking of a possible career? What risks in where you'll live, what schools you'll attend. and what risks, if any, would you like to see your <u>body</u> taking? (Mountain climbing?)

Write about it.

### 90.  (Future Career Thoughts)

Have you given any thought to what career you might be interested in?

Of course, you have <u>lots</u> of time to think about it, and it's really important to enjoy being a KID for many more years, but have you looked at people doing their jobs and thought, "I'd like to do <u>that</u> job"?

Some people choose a career by process of elimination—seeing jobs that they definitely <u>don't</u> want to do, and eliminating from there. Are there jobs you see people doing—like teaching, or being a doctor or firefighter—that you know you'd hate? Or is there a whole range of other jobs that you <u>can</u> imagine yourself doing? What are those?

Maybe, though, you're one of those people who knows <u>exactly</u> what you want to do and have known from about age <u>one</u>. If so, what is <u>that</u> job?

Write about these things.

### 91.  (A Moment When Everything Changed)

Has there been a moment in your life when you knew everything was changed forever?

Sometimes those moments are very large and difficult: parents divorcing, an accident, or some huge bad news. Other times they're very large and pleasurable: winning a prize for something you did, turning a certain age, or moving away from a bad situation.

Sometimes those "nothing will ever be the same" moments are not so large, but still important: someone said something to you that changed everything, or you made an error that forced you to think in a way that you'd never thought before.

What was that important moment?

Write about it.

## 92. (How Do You Best Learn?)

You know yourself: your quirks and your habits. So you probably know how you <u>learn</u> best.

Different students learn best in different ways. Some like to listen to lectures, take notes, and learn by remembering lectures and reviewing their notes. Others like to work in groups and think that working with classmates makes learning more exciting and <u>permanent</u>. Others learn visually—with their eyes—and like things they can <u>look at</u>; they tend to remember those things. Still others like to be able to <u>move around</u> rather than staying in a desk and find that when their <u>body</u> is involved somehow, they learn better.

What about you? What's <u>your</u> best learning style? Can you think of examples of lessons that you learned <u>your way</u>, lessons you still remember?

Write about it.

## 93. (Earliest Memory)

What's your earliest memory?

Some people have <u>amazingly</u> detailed memories: they remember having their diapers changed, standing up in their crib and crying while watching a column of ants climb up the wall, or their mother reading them a story at age one. Others have a difficult time remembering <u>last year</u>, let alone their early years.

Think back: is there one memory that you see in that distant past? What is it? Does it include people speaking to you, or is it just a picture? Does it have other sounds in it—hammers pounding, for example, or people laughing or shouting? What is it?

Are there <u>other</u> ancient memories you can bring up? Do they relate in any way to each other, or are they random?

Write about them.

## 94. (Aspirations Mocked)

Has anyone ever laughed at or made fun of your dreams? No, not the dreams we have when we sleep: dreams of what you want to do with your life.

Sometimes, almost accidentally, kids will blurt out what they'd like to do, and others laugh. Sometimes it takes a while to get up the courage to talk about your life dreams, then others—whether parents or teachers or friends—say, "That's not what you should be! You should be a _____ or a _____!" If you <u>have</u> had someone <u>denigrate</u>

(put down) your dreams, tell about what happened. Tell how you felt when it happened. And did you <u>learn</u> anything from the experience?

Write about it.

## 95.  (What Are You Good at?)

What are you good at, and what could you teach someone?

Oh, lots of people might say, "I'm not really good at anything," but if they really <u>thought</u> about themselves, they'd find things, large and small, that they're good at.

One person might be good at teaching the words to a certain song; another might know a lot about braiding hair; another might be terrific at skateboarding, and another might make an art of simply tying shoes.

How did you get so good at your area—large or small—of expertise, and have you ever taught anyone some or part of your specialty? (If you haven't, how would you teach it?)

Write about it.

## INVENTIONS, INNOVATIONS, AND PASTIMES

## 96.  (Invent a Board Game)

If you were given the challenge to invent a board game—that is, a game that could fit into a flat box and that has a board that folds out or assembles (gets put together from small pieces)—what would you invent?

Would you devise a game that has to do with kids' everyday lives? Would it involve money? Love? Power? Revenge? Peacemaking? Healing?

Would there be figures in your game, that move from place to place? Would there be cars or other objects? Would there be tricky areas that send the player to some kind of board game hell? Would the players have to keep score on a piece of paper?

How would a player <u>win</u> your game?

Write about it.

## 97.  (Invent a Sport)

There are <u>so</u> many sports in the world: soccer and Ping-Pong and football and cricket and badminton and jai alai. <u>So</u> many.

But who says there can't be one more? Who says <u>you</u> can't invent a sport?

Think about a sport you might invent. The sport might involve a ball or not. It might involve equipment such as rackets, sticks, gloves, or any common or odd item.

How will your sport be played? Will it be a team sport, like soccer, or an individual sport, like swimming? What will the rules be? How will a person or team win? What will your sport be called?

Write about it.

## 98.   (Invent a Video Game)

We all know that (much to teachers' chagrin!) kids spend <u>lots</u> of time playing video games. And companies spend millions of dollars developing games to sell to kids.

What if <u>you</u> were offered the chance to invent a video game? What kind of game would you invent? What would the rules be? What characters—animal or human—would be in it? How would the difficulty-levels differ? How would a person score points? Win?

And what would you call it? (Who knows, maybe your game will catch on!)

Write about it.

## 99.   (Invent Something Useful for Your House)

If you could invent something that would be <u>really</u> useful <u>around the house</u>, what would you invent?

Yes, we have vacuum cleaners and blenders and light-dimmers. But what is it that <u>has not</u> been invented and that <u>you'd</u> like to invent? Your invention can be practical—say, an automatic egg peeler—or really goofy and silly.

Tell about your great household invention, and make a case for why it's needed!

## 100.   (One Invention to Help the World)

If you could invent <u>one</u> invention that would help the world in some way, what would you come up with?

Some kids might write about a <u>transportation</u> invention—a cool new car or train—while others might come up with an invention that helps human health. Still others might devise a new form of pollution control, or even something small and really helpful to kids in school.

What do you think? Tell all about your invention, and tell us why it'd be such a great innovation.

## PERSONAL HABITS AND SELF-IDENTIFICATION

### 101.   (What Artist Would You Be?)

<u>Painters</u> use watercolors or acrylic or oil paint or other materials. <u>Sculptors</u> use clay or metal or wood or other materials to make strange and wonderful things. <u>Photographers</u> take pictures, <u>writers</u> write, <u>dancers</u> dance, <u>filmmakers</u> make movies, <u>musicians</u> make music, and a whole range of other artists do terrifically creative things.

If <u>you</u> could be an artist—perhaps you already are!—what type of artist would you be? Even if you think you don't have talent (everyone has <u>some</u> talents!), what sort of artist can you imagine being?

And within that discipline (painting, sculpture, etc.), what do you see yourself doing? Paintings of people? Cool shapes? Dances celebrating freedom? Films about falling in love?

Write about yourself as an artist, real or imagined. Describe what you'd make.

### 102.   (What Habits Do You Have?)

Everyone has habits. Some people have just a <u>few</u> habits—like putting on their left shoe first every morning, or knocking their toothbrush exactly four times on the sink after brushing—and other people have many.

Think about your daily routine. What are <u>your</u> habits? Do they involve the usual things such as dressing and grooming and eating, or do they also include other quirky habits—habits that you're comfortable with and don't seem to want to change?

Write about your habits—even the crazy ones.

### 103.   (Optimist or Pessimist)

Would you say you are an optimist or a pessimist? An optimist is someone who sees the world in a <u>positive</u> light and believes things will come out fine. A pessimist, on the other hand, sees things in a <u>negative</u> way and tends to think that things aren't going well at all. (It's often said that the optimist sees the glass as "half full," while the pessimist sees that same glass as "half empty.")

What about you? Which way do you think you view the small and large things in life? Do you have an optimist's "this is great" attitude, or are you more in the pessimists' camp, thinking, "This is not OK at all!"

Write about it.

### 104.   (What Junk Is Your Treasure?)

One's person's <u>junk</u> is another person's <u>treasure</u>. And one's treasure is another's junk. It's an odd world, but things seem to come out even.

What do you have that you consider a treasure that other kids or adults might consider junk? What makes that thing or those things so special to you? Does it have sentimental value—that is, it gives you special feelings or brings up memories? What's so great about it?

On the other hand, are there things in the world—whether in the world of your house or the wider world—that people seem to treasure and that you think are junk? What are those things? Why do you think they're junk?

Write about these things.

### 105.   (Secret Hiding Place)

Many people have a secret hiding place—a place where important things can be stashed away. Often that secret hiding place is in their own house, but sometimes it's not—sometimes it's in another special place.

Do <u>you</u> have a secret hiding place? If you're trusting enough to tell, where is it? How did it become your secret hiding place? Did you discover it? Does anyone else know about it? Has it always been safe, or has it been discovered?

Finally, do you think it's important for people to have secret hiding places? Why? Write about it.

### 106.   (Special Location)

Do you have a special place in the world that you like a lot, or even love? Maybe it's a place by the water that you visit once in a while when you need to think, or a place where you like to spend time when you feel <u>great</u>. Maybe your special spot is a certain bench in a park where there's a lovely view. Maybe it's a place none of us would guess—an intersection, for example. Or maybe it's your own room.

Tell about your special place: where it is, what it looks like, and why it's so special to you. (You don't need to give the <u>exact</u> location away if you don't want!)

### 107.   (Unforgettable Moment)

Is there a moment in your life that you would characterize as <u>unforgettable</u>? A moment that pops into your mind more than once in a while?

Maybe it was only a "momentito"—a tiny moment when someone said something to you or you said something to someone else—but it's stayed with you somehow.

Or maybe the unforgettable moment was larger: a great success or surprise, or something sadder: a moment of grief or shock that you can never forget.

Write about that indelible moment, and fill us in with sharp details.

### 108. (Being Alone)

How are you at being <u>alone</u>?

Some people can't stand being alone: it scares them, for some reason, and they do everything they can to make sure they're rarely alone. Others <u>love</u> being alone, and try to be alone as much as possible. Still others <u>are</u> alone a lot, and wish they weren't alone so much. And those whose personalities or whose jobs seem to surround them with other people often <u>wish</u> they had more "alone time."

What about you? Are you someone who loves being alone, hates it, or is balanced in the middle? Do you wish you had more alone time, or less? What do you do when you're alone—and how are you feeling? Peaceful? Nervous?

Write about it, alone in your thoughts.

### 109. (Timeliness)

Do you consider yourself an "on time" person? That is, are you usually (always?) on time for school, for appointments, and when you meet people?

Is being on time important to you? If so, why is it important? Does being on time have any life lessons in it, or is it just "being on time"?

How'd you get into the habit? From your parents? Yourself?

If you're <u>not</u> an "on time" person, is there a reason? Is planning a problem for you? Do you think that being late sends a message to people? If so, what? And how did <u>you</u> get into the habit? Your parents? Yourself?

Write about it, either now or a few seconds later.

### 110. (Meditation on Our Bodies)

OK, we have these bodies. We're born with them and carry them around with us every day.

What do you like about your body, and what are you not so crazy about? Do you particularly like your legs, for example—those strong horses that carry you around every day? Are you attached to your quick brain? ;-) On the other hand, so to speak, do you wish your eyes were a little sharper or your arms a little stronger?

And what about <u>accepting</u> your body: are there things about your body that don't look like the handsome male and female bodies seen in television and magazine ads, but that you accept, and even <u>love</u>, anyway?

Finally, how important is a person's body to who that person <u>is</u>—to his or her identity?

Write about your body.

## 111.   (A Must-Read Book)

If there was <u>one</u> book that you'd like to tell people they <u>must</u> read, what book would that be for you?

Sometimes students choose famous old books—the classics, like <u>A Tale of Two Cities</u> or even the Bible, but often students choose favorite books that might not be as famous: <u>The Giver</u>, for example, or <u>The Diary of Anne Frank</u>.

What book do <u>you</u> want to tell the world about? What's it about, and why do you think it's so good? And why should everybody read it, anyway—what good would it do them?

Write about it.

## 112.   (Comfort Food)

Food writers sometimes use the term <u>comfort food</u>. Comfort food is food that makes us feel good when we eat it: it gives us a cozy, homey feeling.

Do <u>you</u> have a "comfort food"—a food that you love to eat, at certain times of the year, or when you're feeling stress? If so, what is that food? Why do you think it's comfort food for you? Is there something in your past that gives you that feeling, or maybe something in your present? What triggers that warm feeling when you eat this food?

Write about it.

## 113.   (Relationship with Anger)

Anger can come from lots of sources: things that happened (or <u>didn't</u> happen) to you in your childhood, frustration, inability to do things, lots of reasons.

Some people have a lot of anger inside them. Some don't have much. Some people let their anger get away from them, and some use their anger as a <u>fuel</u> to do important things.

How much anger do you think you have inside of <u>you</u>? Where do you think your anger comes from—what cause? How do you handle your anger—do you explode, like a firecracker, or do you "see your anger coming," say "hello" to it, and handle it? Do you ever think you use your anger as a fuel—as a tool to be passionate about doing things <u>well</u>?

Write about anger—<u>your</u> anger.

### 114. (Anger Triggers)

It's doubtful that there's anyone in the world who hasn't been angry. Some people become angry often; others, seldom. Some are good at controlling their anger. Others are terrible at it.

What makes <u>you</u> angry? Is there one primary thing, or do many things make you angry? Can you give examples?

Are you pretty good at controlling your anger, or not so good? Do you use strategies to control your anger, such as counting to ten before you speak or strike, or are you just naturally able to control it? Have you ever "lost it," and uncontrollably said some words or struck out at another person? How did you feel after your outburst? Relieved? Guilty? Ashamed?

Finally, what advice would you give other kids that would help them control their anger?

Write about it.

### 115. (Anger Justified?)

Are there some "good" (justified) reasons to get angry and some "bad" (unjustified) ones?

In your own life, as you think back on your own causes of anger, which ones, if any, seemed appropriate, and which ones inappropriate?

Is it justified that someone who's had a hard life slugs another kid who accidentally bumped into him in the hall? Is it justified for a person to get angry at someone who calls her names? Is it justified to get angry at someone whom you <u>heard</u> gossiped about you?

When is anger justified, and when is it not? Is anger something you can control at all? Can your parents teach you how to deal with anger? Can your teachers? Or is anger control something we have to teach ourselves?

Write about it.

### 116. (Room as Reflection of Self)

Some people say that a person's room is a reflection of who he or she is. Others say that's a bunch of baloney—a room is a room, simple as that.

What's <u>your</u> room like? Do you think it's a reflection of your personality, an <u>extension</u> of your personality, or just a room? Do you share it with brothers or sisters, or maybe adults? If so, are you able to make a little "place of your own" amid that shared space, or is that impossible?

Is your room neat and tidy? Is it a little messy? Is it a <u>disaster</u>? What does it all mean?

Write about your room.

### 117. (Worry)

Are you a worrier?

Some people worry about every little thing: what to wear that day, what to eat, whether to walk briskly or slowly, whether to say hello to someone or walk past them—everything.

Other people worry very little, or <u>choose</u> the things to worry about. They try to worry only about the big, important things.

Where are <u>you</u> in this spectrum? Are you a big-time worrier, or do you keep your cool about most things? (Or are you one of those people who <u>look</u> as if they don't worry, but really do!?)

And if you do worry, what do you worry about?

Write about it.

### 118. (Biggest Fear)

Worry is one thing. But what about <u>fear</u>? What's your biggest fear?

Psychologists tell us that, perhaps because of television reports, fear of being kidnapped is prominent in kids' minds. (The reality is that you have a <u>very</u> small chance of ever being kidnapped. But just because it probably won't happen doesn't mean kids aren't afraid, does it?) Students themselves sometimes report that they fear failure, being alone for a long time, or being abandoned.

Every person has a few big fears, but what is your "number one"?

Write about it, and, if you can, think about and write about why you're afraid of that thing, and where you think your fear might have come from.

### 119. (How Have You Changed?)

How have you changed over the years?

Of course, we all <u>grow</u> physically, up and out, and that's worth writing about. But we all change in different ways. One person, for example, might have been a big complainer or cry baby in his early years, and now takes things coolly and doesn't let much bother him. Another person might have had <u>no</u> interest in science in elementary school, and now her scientific interest is blossoming, <u>exploding</u>.

Social change is important, too. Shy people become less shy sometimes, and, alas, sometimes people who were extremely <u>happy</u> in earlier years become rather unhappy.

Where are <u>you</u> in this change spectrum? Write about it.

### 120. (Relationship with Silence)

Silence. Nothing can be heard.

What's your relationship with silence? Does it make you uncomfortable, or do you enjoy it? When you're talking with a friend, for example, and the two of you fall into silence, do you feel compelled (pushed to) fill in the silence, even if you're not saying much? Or are you comfortable with that silence?

Do you have <u>enough</u> silence in your life, or not enough? Where do you <u>get</u> silence: do you go somewhere to find it, or do you have it at home much of the time? Do you ever try to <u>get away</u> from silence? Why? And do you think silence is good for us, as people, or not so good?

Write about it.

### 121. (Advice to a Younger Self)

If you could give advice to <u>yourself</u>—that self two or three years younger—what advice would you give? This is the old, "If I knew then what I know now," issue, meaning that we <u>really</u> learn by experience.

What advice would you give yourself, standing beside that younger version of <u>you</u>? Would you give advice on how to get along socially? Academically, in school? Psychologically (in the head—"attitude"), how to cope, how to deal with things that come up in life? Things definitely to do? Things <u>not</u> to do?

Write about it, and give yourself some good advice.

## 122.   (I Wish This Didn't Happen)

There are lots of things in life that <u>we wish didn't happen</u>. Some things we have control of, but many are completely out of our control.

What is one thing you wish didn't happen?

Perhaps that thing was a world-affecting event: global warming, or the atomic bombs on Hiroshima and Nagasaki, for example. Or perhaps that thing was our own personal atomic bomb: something that happened in our lives that we wish we could erase. Maybe we had control over the way it went, or maybe we just observed, completely impotent (without power).

Write about it, and if you can, write about how we—or you—can move on with life, using that event as a <u>lesson</u> from which to learn.

## 123.   (Important Family Photo)

Is there a <u>photograph</u> that you or your family has taken that means a lot to you?

Maybe the photograph is of terrific quality—an enlarged family portrait—or maybe it's of relatively poor quality—a small, badly focused snapshot taken at a birthday party, for example. It's not the <u>quality</u> of the picture we're talking about here, it's the <u>content</u>.

What is it in that photograph that means something to you? Are there people in it who are (were?) important to you? Are there details in it—things in the background, an expression on someone's face, perhaps, that move you emotionally, or trigger further memories?

Write about that photograph. Be as detailed as possible, and be sure to talk about <u>why</u> it's important to you.

## 124.   (Importance of Pets)

How important are pets to you? Some people say dogs and cats are ridiculous—a crutch that people need because they're lonely. <u>They're too much trouble</u>, they say. <u>They don't belong in the city</u>. Other people say that pets can make our lives richer, and that animals can communicate with us in ways that people can't.

Where are <u>you</u> on the pets issue? Do you have a pet, or pets? If not, do you wish you had? (If so, what <u>kind</u> of pet would you like?)

Do you think that pets serve a <u>purpose</u>? What about people: do <u>we</u> serve a purpose to pets? Think about pets—either <u>your</u> pets, or pets in general—and write about them. (Go for description here, and support your ideas where you can.)

### 125. (Importance of Music)

How important is music in your life? Is music—whether instrumental (no singing) or vocal (singing) important to you?

Is music for you simply as it is for some people—a kind of background noise—or is it something more, something you feel deeply, something that thrills?

If music is important, <u>how</u> is it important, and <u>why</u> do you think it's important to you? Does it simply distract you, or does it stir something deeper? What kinds of music "touch" you, and what kinds leave you "cold"? Do you think you're open to listening to other kinds of music, or are you loyal to one type only?

Write about it.

## DREAMS

### 126. (Recurrent Dreams)

At night, do you sometimes have recurrent dreams? (Something is <u>recurrent</u> when it repeats.)

Some people have the same dream over and over, sometimes easy to understand and sometimes hard. Maybe there's a teenage boy with a white shirt on walking across a grassy field with a baseball glove in his hand, and you dream that scene over and over.

Other people have recurring nightmares, and are afraid when they go to sleep that they'll have "that dream" again.

What about you? Have you had a dream (or dreams) recur? More than once? If so, what was it about? Do you have any idea why you might repeat that dream, and, if you think dreams have meaning, what might it mean?

Write about it.

### 127. (Meaning of Dreams)

Are you a person who believes that nighttime dreams have meaning and that objects and people and animals in our dreams have symbolism?

Many famous psychologists—Carl Jung among them—spent their entire careers studying dreams, writing books about their meanings, giving speeches about what dreams mean, and helping people understand their dreams.

Others say that dreams don't bear much meaning—that they're just the brain's way of exercising while the body's asleep.

What do you think? Do dreams have meaning? Do you think you've had dreams that related to your waking life? If so, what do you think they meant?

Write about it.

## 128. (Nightmares)

Everyone has nightmares: about monsters in the middle of the night, horrible situations you can't seem to escape, falling from high places, friends or loved ones in trouble. Everyone has awakened from nightmares and sat up in bed so glad they weren't real.

Do you have nightmares very often? What are they? How do you handle them: Are you able to talk to the nightmares in your dreams—confront them—or do you wake up in a sweat? Do you think your nightmares relate to any fears you might have? Do you have any strategies to conquer those nightmares (or those fears)?

Write about them.

## 129. (Sweet Dreams)

Indonesian people sometimes say mimpi manis before they go to bed. Mimpi manis means "sweet dreams." Lots of cultures, in fact, wish "sweet dreams" to loved ones.

Do you have "sweet dreams" sometimes—dreams that are so delightful that you wish they'd never end, and when you wake up you're disappointed that they weren't real? Does that dream ever come back to you? Are you able to will your dream to come back, and have it come back—whether that same night or another?

What is the sweetest dream you've ever had? Why did you like it so much? Do you think it had any symbolism in your everyday life, or was it just delightful and nothing more?

Write about it.

## 130. ("Planted" Dreams)

If you had the power to "plant" nighttime dreams in a friend's or loved one's head, what dreams would you plant?

Would you plant a dream in a parent's head that they took you to Disneyland, or Jamaica, or Paris, and had a GREAT time—hoping that they'd wake and plan a vacation there next summer? Would you plant a trick dream in a friend's cranium, or maybe a romantic dream in someone else's?

Describe the dream-seeds you'd sow, and the happy (unhappy?) recipients.

### 131.   (Daydreaming)

Are you a daydreamer?

Of course, teachers like to think that <u>all</u> of their kids are paying attention <u>all</u> the time, but perhaps the reality is a little different.

What, first, are the <u>situations</u> in which you find yourself daydreaming? Maybe riding in a car, or sitting in your room, or in a quiet (<u>boring</u>?) class?

And what do you daydream about? Do your thoughts travel a predictable course—thinking about <u>basketball</u> for a while, then thinking about <u>mathematical equations</u> or <u>clowns</u>? Or do they travel another "track"? Or do your thoughts fly randomly, like birds in flight? Where do those thought-birds go?

Write about it.


## DEEP LIFE ISSUES

### 132.   (Love, Defined)

People write about love all the time, but they almost never define it.

Can love <u>be</u> defined? Can a person say, "Well, love, of course, is _____ and _____, with a little of _____ mixed in." (Would a simple formula like that satisfy you?)

What <u>is</u> love, anyway? Can you describe it? What does it look like? What does it feel like? Smell like? Sound like? Taste like?

Where does a person find it if she or he is looking for it? Is it in a certain place? Does it have certain habits or routines? If so, what are those? Is it hard to get? Easy to get? Do you need to be qualified to get it? Is there anyone who <u>doesn't</u> have it? Is there anyone who <u>can't</u> have it? Is there anyone who has <u>too much</u> of it? Is it something people eventually want to get rid of, like day-old fish?

Write about love.


### 133.   (Different Kinds of Love)

If you were to focus on <u>love</u> today, and your job was to tell the world about <u>different kinds of love</u>, what would you say? Is all love the same between people, or is love different in every relationship? If it's different, what are those differences?

Can the types of love change, or does each type stay the same forever? Are the types of love <u>useful</u> to people—either to people personally, or to our society?

Write about love, and its differences.

### 134. (Crushes)

Some adults say that teenagers with "crushes" on each other are going through "puppy love." That's a way of saying that it isn't as <u>important</u> as love among adults.

What do you think about that? Do you think that when two teenagers "fall in love" their love is as important as love in adults? Since you're not an adult, it might be difficult to answer this next question, but do you think it's as <u>powerful</u> as adult love?

What do you notice in romantic love among adults that is different from romantic love in teenagers? Do the feelings seem different? More intense? Less? Do you think that teenage love might burn hotter than love among adults? Is every situation different?

Write about it.

### 135. (Wisdom, Defined)

What is wisdom?

Is wisdom getting all 4.0s on report cards, or graduating with a Ph.D. from a terrific university? Is it rising quickly to the top of a great corporation? Is it possessing a photographic memory?

Or is wisdom something else—something that a person cannot take a <u>test</u> for? Can people without "qualifications" have wisdom? If so, how do they get it?

Finally, do you know a person or people whom you consider wise? How old are they? (Does being <u>wise</u> necessitate being <u>old</u>?) What do these people <u>do</u> or <u>say</u> to make you think they're wise?

Write about it.

### 136. (What Is Forgiveness?)

What is your idea of what <u>forgiveness</u> is?

Is forgiveness something that should be practiced often, or should a person only practice forgiveness once in a while?

Have there been times in your life when <u>you</u> have practiced forgiveness? What were those times? Are there other times when you <u>wanted</u> to practice forgiveness, but somehow could not? Why were you not able to? (Are there some insults or outrages for which you find it impossible to forgive a person? What are those things, and why do you think you're unable to forgive in those circumstances? Are there people who forgive <u>everyone</u> for <u>everything</u>? Does that seem wise and mature to you?)

Write about these things.

### 137. (Families: Love Apportionment)

In a family, does everyone get the same quantity (amount) and quality of love?

It's difficult to measure love (how would you measure it, anyway?), but do all parents and children get exactly the same amount of love from other members of the family?

What about the quality of love: does each family member get the same quality of love as others, or do certain family members get "better" love?

Do you think that most kids think that other siblings are getting more love, or better love, than they? Is that just part of being a kid?

And what about siblings' loving each other? Are the qualities and quantities of love all the same, or do you think they differ?

Write about it.

### 138. (Experience with Death)

Death is something we have to live with. It can be slow or quick, painful or painless. Thankfully, none of us in this class can say we've experienced death, but have you had experience with death?

Perhaps an adult friend or a distant relative or a grandparent died. Some kids, sadly, even have had the tragedy of having closer family members die: perhaps a parent or a brother or sister.

Do you think about death sometimes? Do you think about a person (or persons) you knew who died? What are your thoughts, then? Do you remember moments from, say, their lives, or do you remember other things?

Write about it, if you want.

### 139. (Someone Who Died)

Is there someone in your family—or perhaps even a friend—who has died, and about whom you have never written?

If so, maybe today's the day to write about him or her. Maybe today you'd like to detail in your journal who that person was, what he or she was like, and what you loved (maybe even didn't love?) about him or her.

Often in thinking about those who have "passed on" it helps focus our thinking when we relate (tell about) a particular incident that we remember about the dead person, or a particular thing he or she said to us. You might consider doing that.

Think a little, and write about that person.

### 140. (Understanding Death)

Of all things in the human experience, death is one of the hardest to understand.

What do you think death is all about? Why do we die—for some purpose, maybe, or is death perhaps nature's way of making room for more people on the earth?

What happens after we die? Some people believe that there is a soul, and that the soul goes to a place called <u>heaven</u>. Some believe in hell, others believe we are reincarnated as a person, an animal, a flower, etc., and still others believe that there's simply <u>nothing</u> after death.

What about you? What do you think? Is there an afterlife, or is it all over upon death? Are you confused, like so many of us?

Write about it.

### 141. (Communicating with the Dead)

As you probably know, Halloween originally was the <u>eve</u>—a celebration like Christmas Eve—of All Hallows Day, a day honoring the dead. Other celebrations of the dead occur elsewhere in the world: <u>El Dia de los Muertos</u> for one example.

Some people say that once people die, they're gone; there's nothing left; it's over. Others believe that one way or another the dead remain with us—that we can even communicate with their spirits.

What do you think about communication with the dead? Do you believe in it? Indeed, do you think that there <u>is</u> such a thing as a <u>soul</u>? If so, can it be communicated with after the body dies? What makes you believe what you do? Have you had someone you know die and "felt" them afterward—felt that you "got in touch" with their spirit?

And what about spirits <u>not</u> related to you, or <u>ghosts</u>? Do they exist? If so, what are they, and what makes you think they exist?

Write about these things.

### 142. (Litany of Deep Questions)

The world has so many mysteries, both about the way we live our lives and the physical world. Where does illness come from? Why do some people live short lives and others long? Are mean people ever sorry that they're mean? Is the universe expanding or contracting? Why do we think things are beautiful?

So many questions. We all have them. Sometimes they get answered, and sometimes not.

How about you? What kinds of questions do <u>you</u> have about human life or human behavior or the physical world?

See if you can come up with one <u>huge</u> paragraph filled with every question that comes to your mind. (Don't try to answer them: just ask them, even if they seem silly!)

### 143. (Defining Courage)

What is courage?

Is courage chasing a bank robber down the street until he's caught? Is courage shooting down an enemy plane from a hideout on a mountaintop?

Or can courage be other things, too: a handicapped person making her way down the street in her wheelchair, or a father working twelve hours a day in a horrible job to pay the rent and feed his children? Does a courageous person have to be an adult?

How do <u>you</u> define courage? Do you know anyone in your own life whom you'd define as courageous? Why would you call that person courageous?

Write about it.

### 144. (Hate Defined)

What is <u>hate</u>, anyway? Is there a difference between <u>dislike</u> and <u>hate</u>? Is there some kind of thermometer we have inside us that tells us when we <u>dislike</u> something and when we <u>hate</u> it? How do we know when we <u>hate</u> something, rather than just <u>dislike</u> it? Does our face burn? Do our bodies tell us?

Some people say that we hate what (or who) we recognize as being something inside ourselves that we don't like. Do you believe that? What function does hate have, anyway? Why do people hate? Does hate help us, as people, or as a society? What does hate do to us, inside ourselves and in our world?

Write about hate.

### 145. (Abuse)

As you probably know, child abuse can happen in a number of forms—physical abuse (including sexual abuse), psychological (mental) abuse, and neglect. (Neglect is failing to take care of someone properly.)

How big a problem do you think child abuse—in any of its forms—is among kids <u>you</u> know? Have you ever known someone who was experiencing any form of child abuse? If so, what did he or she do about it, if anything? (Do <u>you</u> know what to do if you or someone you know is being abused?)

What is <u>your</u> definition of child abuse? What sorts of physical and psychologi-cal abuses and neglect can define child abuse in <u>your</u> opinion? When you talk about psychological abuse, what do you mean? Is psychological abuse verbal cruelty, or can it be other things? Can <u>pressure</u> put on a child be abuse?

Write about it.

## 146. (Happiness Defined)

Would you consider yourself a "happy" person?

What <u>is</u> happiness? Is happiness going around with a smile on our face all day, or is it something else? Are we supposed to be happy all the time we're awake? If so, why? If not, how much time <u>should</u> we be happy? Should we alternate days? Have people given you the feeling that you're supposed to be happy all the time, or do you think it's normal <u>not</u> to be happy sometimes?

Write about it, and give examples where you can.

## 147. (Money Buy Happiness?)

Can money <u>buy</u> happiness?

Some people claim that happiness <u>can</u> be bought: a luxurious car, a fancy house, elegant furniture, all the latest clothes.

But is it true? Do you think that money and happiness are related? Is it possible, for example, to be quite happy and extremely poor? Or, on the other hand, does a person have a <u>much</u> better chance of being happy having a few bucks in her purse and <u>lots</u> of bucks in the bank? (Is it even <u>possible</u> to be unhappy if you're rich?)

Or is there some middle ground: an idea that money really <u>helps</u> as a factor—maybe not the only factor—in happiness?

Write about it.

## 148. (Happiness/Joy Distinctions)

Is there a difference between <u>happiness</u> and <u>joy</u>? Are they the same thing?

When do people (you?) experience happiness? When do they (again, you?) ex-perience joy?

Is happiness there all the time, and is joy just super-happiness? Does joy "weigh" more than happiness? Or is joy something different: something you can't weigh?

How does a person <u>get</u> joy or happiness? Can they buy it? Can they get it from someone else? Does everyone have both happiness and joy?

Write about happiness and joy.

### 149.  (What's Important?)

Some things are important to us from a very early age and stay important all our lives. Other things are important to us for a while, then their importance fades.

What's important to you at this time in your life? What has meaning in your life?

Something as complex as family relationships might be important; making and keeping friends might be important; activities at school or elsewhere might be important; how you're doing in school and planning for your future might occupy you now—or, perhaps, a more eccentric and lovely thing like reading every word of a favorite series of books.

Why do you think these things are important—either to you or generally?

Write about it.


## LAST DAY

### 150.  (Last Journal Entry)

Today's journal entry will be the last one of the year. We need to do a little reflection on how the journals went for you.

In the beginning, when the process was explained (and the grading!) what did you think? Did you think that you'd be able to do well? How were the first weeks for you? A struggle? Easy? Later, what changes did you go through in your attitude about journal?

Looking back on your journal, in what ways do you think your writing has changed over the year? What do you notice about length, sentence structure, relaxation, new words for you, writing confidence, etc. Do you think that your writing has improved? Are you proud of the amount of writing you have done in your journal? Has your journal given you a better sense of who you are?

Finally, what could I improve about journals? Should they be more time? Less? More often? Less often? Are the prompts OK? Should I change the way the whole process is done? (If so, be specific.)

Write about it.

# Selected and Annotated Discography

The following discs are terrific for Fluency Journals. All listings include what I call a "Frenetic Scale," a 1–10 measure reflecting relative calmness to relative craziness. The scale is useful because prompts can be complemented—even energized or deepened—by musical selections, and once in a while, especially after the program is firmly established, it's a lot of fun to put on a well-played frantic piece. So: A "1" on the Frenetic Scale indicates music so slow-paced or low-key that it's almost comatose (though the fact that it's included here means that it's been successful), and a rare piece that receives a "10" on the scale is *very* wild and probably should be used only with classes with whom control is not an issue, and who are so deeply immersed in the process that their entire psyches would thrill that you dared play it.

Selections are classified loosely by genre. If I'm particularly fond of a certain version of, say, a classical piece, I'll mention it. However, some companies produce *very* good renditions of classical music for a great price. (Naxos is one example; their catalogue is now huge, including even contemporary composers. And be sure to check out Nonesuch's Explorer Series for excellence in World Music. Each company has a Web site.)

In some cases, I make recommendations as to which consecutive cuts work best, based on the twenty-minute journal session. If no such recommendations are made, the CD is fine played from the beginning.

Finally, I recognize that hundreds of composers and musicians are not represented in this discography and *should* be here. It's a matter of space, really, and of deciding at a certain point to stop. What's offered here is music that will work with kids. But try your own selections too, watching how kids are reacting—and bearing in mind that some music, love it as you might, works *against* writing.

## CLASSICAL

**Bach, C.P.E.,** *Sonata & Rondos,* **Mikhail Pletnev, Deutsche Grammophon 289 459 614–2. Frenetic Scale: 5**

Pletnev's virtuosity will amaze you, big Bach's best boy's baroque jazz will turn your head, and you'll see a few piano students in the class smile in admiration. Anywhere you start this CD brings awesome rewards.

**Bach, J. S.,** *Bach Organ Book,* **Philip Brunelle, Quintessence CDQ 2020. Frenetic Scale: 6**

This is an inexpensive version of famous Bach organ work—perfectly adequate for the price. Others will serve just as well. Kids are sometimes familiar with a few of the pieces, and most are enthralled with hearing the power here. Multipurpose.

**Bach, J. S.,** *The Goldberg Variations,* **Glenn Gould, CBS Masterworks MK3779. Frenetic Scale: 4**

Legendary recording of *Goldberg* by the eccentric virtuoso Gould. Listen carefully, and you'll hear him humming as he plays. This is the 1970 follow-up to the brilliant version performed in 1955. If this isn't rock and roll, Gould doesn't know what is. (There's another double-set version containing both the '55 and the '70, if you're interested in comparison.)

**Balada, Leonardo,** *Piano Concerto #3, Concierto Magico, Music for Flute and Orchestra,* **Barcelona Symphony and Catalonia National Orchestra, Naxos 8.555039. Frenetic Scale: 2–8**

Spanish contemporary composer Balada writes that his music is a "symbiosis of the past and the future for which [he has] been practicing for thirty years." This fascinating music—three separate compositions, three journal entries—combines Spanish folk elements (Andalusian gypsy strains among them) and modern techniques. Lots of surprises. Once kids are "in the groove," this CD will serve you well.

**Battle, Kathleen, and Marsalis, Wynton, *Baroque Duet,* Sony Classical SK 46672. Frenetic Scale: 3**

In most cases singing and writing don't go together. Here, though, formidable Battle's voice—in languages unfamiliar to most American kids—serves as *instrument,* and doesn't disturb. Marsalis at his usual virtuoso versatility, Battle's thrilling glissades marvelous. Kids deserve to hear great singing. (Handel, Scarlatti, Predieri, Stradella, Bach represented here.)

**Coates, Gloria, *String Quartets Nos. 2, 3, 4, 7, and 8,* Kreutzer Quartet, Naxos 8.559152. Frenetic Scale: 2**

Halloween? Have a creepy prompt on the board? This music by contemporary American Coates will scare the bejabbers out of the kids. (See Jerry Xie's entry in Appendix D.) Coates's string quartets do everything imaginable to catgut and nylon and steel: these sounds contort unbelievably. Reserved for those special eerie, atmospheric prompts. Higher-functioning upper-level kids will thrive on this music; perhaps contraindicated for kids with serious emotional issues.

**Copland, Aaron, *Copland,* Royal Philharmonic Orchestra, Royal Philharmonic/Intersound 2841. Frenetic Scale: 5–9**

A strong version of Copland classics, even played by the British. Begins with "Fanfare for the Common Man," includes "Billy the Kid," "Hoedown," of course, and "Appalachian Spring." "Billy" alone is twenty minutes; a few good journal sessions here.

**Cozzolani, Chiara Margarita, *Messa Paschale,* Magnificat, Musica Omnia mo0209. Frenetic Scale: 2**

Latin sacred music (choral) by seventeenth-century Benedictine nun Cozzolani. This is a mass, but its religiosity is fairly irrelevant in the classroom: wonderful music in female voices—rare in early liturgy. Good for pensive writers dealing with consequential prompts.

**Fauré and Duruflé, *Requiems,* Philharmonia Orchestra, Sony 67182. Frenetic Scale: 2**

Nothing like a beautiful requiem in the air during writing to deeply thoughtful prompts. Vocal work here, but in Latin and not distractive. Lucia Popp is soprano in the Fauré, Kiri Te Kanawa in the Duruflé.

**Gershwin, George,** *Rhapsody in Blue/American in Paris,* **Chicago Symphony, Deutsche Grammophon G2–31625. Frenetic Scale: 6**

James Levin conducting (and on piano). The jazz band version of Gershwin's *Rhapsody,* not at all schmaltzy, as so often occurs. The *Rhapsody* itself goes sixteen minutes, so there's a journal session. *An American in Paris* runs more than seventeen; that can serve another day. (If you've got *Rhapsody* up loud enough, watch the kids' faces during the first few bars. If you play *An American in Paris* early second semester, you'll be laying the groundwork for subsequent Copland and contemporary new composers.)

**Glass, Philip,** *The Photographer,* **CBS MK 37849. Frenetic Scale: 7**

English lyrics in this piece, but few words intelligible. One of contemporary composer Glass's early pieces, repetitive, quite compelling to the kids. They may ask for it again. Suggested in the second semester, when students are accustomed to "weird" music.

**The Harp Consort,** *Missa Mexicana,* **Harmonia Mundi HMU907293. Frenetic Scale: 2–3**

Seventeenth-century Mexican music, incorporating African rhythms and slave songs, "New World" rhythms, and Spanish street music called *xacára.* Go a few tracks in to begin. A crazy mix of musics, some simply majestic.

**Holst, Gustav,** *The Planets,* **London Symphony Orchestra, Laserlight 14010. Frenetic Scale: 2–7**

Full orchestral movie-sound-like grandiosity, only Pluto and Earth missing. Want a quiet start? Begin with Venus, Track 2.

**Jarrett, Keith,** *The Köln Concert,* **ECM 1064/65 810 067–2. Frenetic Scale: Varying, 2–8**

Classical? Jazz? Hard to know. Jarrett's brilliant piano *tour de force* improv in 1975, the first cut alone going twenty-six minutes. Deeply personal, sometimes perhaps a little narcissistic, but exquisite in its sonority, tone, and unexpected directions. Great for introspective prompts.

**Kabalevsky and Prokofiev, *Russian Soul*, Daniel Shafran, cello, Cello Classics 67575453162. Frenetic Scale: 4–6**

Stirring renditions of Kabalevsky's passionate Concerto for Cello #2 Op. 77 and Prokofiev's Symphony/Concerto for Cello and Orchestra in E minor. Daniel Shafran *blazes* on the cello. Kids listen carefully to this music.

**Kronos Quartet, *Early Music (Lachrymae Antiquae)*, Nonesuch 79457–2. Frenetic Scale: 1**

A *very* strange and mesmerizing collection by these innovators, consisting of twenty-one lugubrious "early music" pieces, some composed as early as the ninth century, others contemporary versions of early music, including composers such as John Cage. The tone may be low, the tempo slow, but there's not a moment of *ennui* on this CD. Lots of impressive rumination will grow from this work.

**Les Nouveaux Musiciens, *Quartets & Duos for Bassoon*, Harmonia Mundi HMN 911788. Frenetic Scale: 2–5**

Five eighteenth-century pieces for bassoon—tight, attentive playing by Laurent Lefévre. Viola, cello, and violin accompaniment. The sound is so good you can even hear Lefévre's keys tapping.

**Mozart, Wolfgang Amadeus, *Complete Piano Concertos Volume 2*, Jenö Jandó, Concentus Hungaricus, Naxos 8.5500202. Frenetic Scale: 3–4**

Another inexpensive Naxos CD, this volume containing three of Mozart's most famous piano concertos. Each concerto goes a little past the twenty-minute writing period, but at least the kids will get a representative taste of Mozart's energy and range before the year is out.

**Pärt, Arvo, *Fratres*, Hungarian State Opera Orchestra, Naxos/8.553750. Frenetic Scale: 3**

The most widely played of contemporary composer Pärt's work. Moody, deep, sonorous; bass-heavy strains rise into strident violins. Good for contemplative prompt.

**Rodrigo, Joaquin, and Villa-Lobos, Heitor,** *Concierto de Aranjuez, Guitar Concerto,* **Julian Bream, RCA Victor Gold Seal 07863565252. Frenetic Scale: 3**

Master guitarist Bream with these familiar and elegant concertos. New to the kids' ears, probably, and always a delight for teachers as well. Guitar work rapid in places, but frenetic scale nonetheless low. Good choice for more placid prompts.

**Satie, Eric,** *Gymnopédies, et al.,* **Ronan O'Hora, Royal Philharmonic/Intersound 2853. Frenetic Scale: 2**

Another inexpensive version. A thoughtful, even sad prompt can't be better accompanied than with Satie, either Gymnopédies or Gnossiennes, both on this CD. I often start the year with Satie.

**Schubert, Franz,** *Death and the Maiden,* **Amadeus Quartet, Deutsche Grammophon 447 611 2. Frenetic Scale: 5**

Stirring version of Schubert's String Quartet in D minor. Brilliant, assertive first few notes will galvanize the kids. Long-time winner for me, especially in lively prompts. Lots of depth here, though, and implicit story.

**Tchaikovsky, Pëter Ilich,** *Swan Lake,* **Boston Symphony Orchestra, Seiji Ozawa Conducting, Deutsche Grammophon. Frenetic Scale: 4**

Why not expose kids to the full *Swan Lake,* instead of the excerpts so many of us are accustomed to? (Certainly, the latter is better than nothing, but this version is wonderful, and many journal days can arise from it.)

**Various Composers,** *Lamentations,* **Oxford Camerata, Naxos 8.550572. Frenetic Scale: 2**

Choral music, in Latin, so not disturbing to journal-writers. Quiet sixteenth-century music, good for thoughtful prompts.

**Vivaldi, Antonio,** *Various Works,* **Berliner Philharmoniker with Nigel Kennedy, EMI Classic 7243 5 57666 01. Frenetic Scale: 4–5**

A blistering attack on Vivaldi, Kennedy's famously energetic violin. Tracks 4–15, "The Four Seasons," is a fine version for kids to be exposed to. (I love his interpretation of "Summer.") A wonderful "Concerto for 2 Violins in D." Three journal days from this CD, and a good opportunity to convince kids, if only aurally, that classical music can rock.

# JAZZ AND OTHER AMERICAN

**Bechet, Sidney, et al.,** *Sidney Bechet,* **BMG 6590–2-RB. Frenetic Scale: 7**

Ho, boy. This is Bechet, but also features The New Orleans Feetwarmers, Tommy Ladnier, Jelly Roll Morton, and Dr. Henry Levine. Great 1930s and early 1940s templates of our jazz heritage, Bechet's trademark trill will interest, and perhaps thrill, the kids. (Track 7 includes funny lyrics, but will disturb journal-writers.) Maybe think about starting on Track 8. Check out "The Mooche," Track 19, and the absolutely *raucous* "Twelfth Street Rag" (Track 20).

**Brubeck, Dave, Quartet,** *Time Out,* **Columbia CK 40585. Frenetic Scale: Varying, 2–7**

The liner notes on this classic album say Brubeck blends "three cultures: the formalism of classical Western music, the freedom of jazz improvisation, and the often complex pulse of African folk music." Solid jazz, lovely bridges. "Take Five" might even be familiar to a few kids.

**Coltrane, John,** *My Favorite Things,* **Atlantic 1361–2. Frenetic Scale: 4**

Tracks 1 and 2 of this seminal magnificence (McCoy Tyner, piano, Steve Davis, bass, Elvin Jones, drums) will last almost an entire journal session, Tracks 3 and 4 (higher Frenetic Scale) another one. Kids shouldn't leave your room in June without being exposed to some Coltrane.

**Coltrane, John,** *The Ultimate Blue Train,* **Blue Note 7243 4 95324 2 7. Frenetic Scale: 2–8**

Another famous one. Coltrane on sax, Lee Morgan on trumpet. Tracks 1 and 2 alone serve for a good journal entry. Preview this one to fit tracks with the energy you want.

**Davis, Miles,** *Kind of Blue,* **Columbia CK 64935. Frenetic Scale: 3–7**

What to say? Miles, Adderly, Coltrane, Kell, Evans, Chambers, Cobb. One of the most important jazz CDs in existence. Another "must play" before the kids leave you. (Make sure they get a taste of "All Blues" [Track 4] before they hit the door.)

**Evans, Bill,** *Waltz for Debbie,* **Riverside OJCCD-210–2 (RLP-9399). Frenetic Scale: 4**

One of great jazz pianist Evans's most famous collections, also one of the best. Of interest on this CD is the fact that three takes are repeated in different versions. His "Porgy" must be one of the most tender recorded.

**Haden, Charlie, and Metheny, Pat,** *Beyond the Missouri Sky,* **Verve 314 537 130–2. Frenetic Scale: 2**

I've played this CD a hundred times and never get tired of it. Haden and Metheny call these songs "short stories," and they really play that way. A few journal sessions here: very evocative, exquisitely beautiful, Haden on bass and Metheny on guitar. Anywhere you start this CD will entrance the kids. (Be sure the kids get to hear the last track, "Spiritual"; play it once for the class and once again for yourself after they leave. *This* is what we're involved in when we teach: *this* beauty, difficult as it can be.)

**Hawkins, Coleman,** *Body & Soul,* **BMG 09026 68515–2. Frenetic Scale: 4**

Unforgettable 1940s jazz classics. The mere three minutes of "Body and Soul" seems a long, lovely dream. This is one of those albums that you hope lodge in the kids' unconscious somewhere, to be resurrected as conscious appreciation many years later.

**Henderson, Joe,** *The Definitive Joe Henderson,* **Verve 314 589 840–2. Frenetic Scale: 4**

Sax man Henderson lovely here, solid sidemen. If you want to have a relatively slow and "cool" session, start with Track 4, "Mode for Joe." Your twenty-minute session will give the kids a taste of accomplished tenor sax. Other cuts fine, too, quicker in tempo. "Lush Life" particularly wonderful.

**Joplin, Scott,** *Piano Rags,* **Joshua Rifkin, Nonesuch 79159. Frenetic Scale: 3**

These old rags wear well, and it would be a shame if, in a series of jazz pieces, the kids were not exposed to Joplin's important—sometimes familiar—and seminal work. Start anywhere: at least two good sessions from this collection, cleanly played by Rifkin.

**Marsalis, Wynton,** *Carnaval,* **Eastman Wind Ensemble, CBS Records MK 42137. Frenetic Scale: 5**

Not what you might expect from Marsalis. This is American wind-band music from the Civil War era to the 1920s, Marsalis on cornet. Trumpeter and cornetist Marshall Johnson tells me that this music was "bandstand" music during those days, avidly heard by hundreds in small towns across America. Part of our history, music unlikely to be heard by kids otherwise.

**McFerrin, Bobby,** *beyond words,* **Blue Note/Angel 7243 5 34201 2 3. Frenetic Scale: 5**

McFerrin's gentle vocals with Chick Corea on piano and Richard Bona on bass make this perfect for a day of calm. You can sense a love for melodic experiment here, delicately delivered.

**Mingus, Charles,** *Blue & Roots,* **Atlantic/Rhino R2 75205. Frenetic Scale: 8**

Some of the best jazz ever: hard-driving, ferocious work. Perfect for an energetic prompt, spring semester, in an on-task, music-craving class. Want to start slowly and wind up? Begin at Track 2. Shoot for the skies immediately? Start with Track 1. You'll get three terrific sessions from this CD, your student audiophiles appreciating the sensational stereo separation. Warning: there's some hootin' and hollerin' in this CD: the sound of musicians having a great time. Will distract the kids, but only briefly.

**Modern Jazz Quartet,** *Django,* **Prestige OJCCD-057–2. Frenetic Scale: 3**

Classic, classy MJQ 1950s work. A chance for the kids to hear Milt Jackson on vibes, John Lewis on piano, Percy Heath on bass, and Kenny Clarke on drums. Good for a gray day when the air moves slowly and the kids do, too.

**Monk, Thelonius,** *Monk's Greatest Hits,* **Columbia/Legacy CK 65422. Frenetic Scale: 4–7**

Hard to imagine exposing the kids to jazz without giving them a little taste of Monk. (Wait till the musicians in the class get an earful of "Misterioso.") Just the first two cuts on this CD will fill a journal session. For a slightly lower-tempo session, go from Track 6 to Track 8. (Note: if you want to *introduce* a long series of "jazz days" in journal, you might put Monk's "Straight, No Chaser" on right off: Track 9.

**Spence, Bill, with Fennig's All Star String Band,** *The Hammered Dulcimer,* **Front Hall Records FHR 302CD. Frenetic Scale: 2–6**

Subtitled "42 Country Dance Tunes," this sixty-five-minute compilation isn't simply hammered dulcimer work; it's the full band playing what string man Richard Shaw calls "all the old timey stuff—waltzes, reels, jigs & shuffles." English and Irish tunes here, too, and the wonderful John Pederson on banjo. The kids *will* stay in their seats on this one, but only because of the layered years of coercion. Watch their feet, though: they're happy, *and they're comin' in your direction.*

**Tatum, Art,** *Piano Starts Here,* **Columbia CK64690. Frenetic Scale: 2–4**

Rather hissy remastering of very old pieces of great improviser Tatum from 1949. Kids should be exposed to this precursor—some funny cuts here, especially his rendition of "Humoresque."

**Terry, Clark,** *In Orbit,* **Riverside 12–271 Original Jazz Classics. Frenetic Scale: 5**

Solid American jazz from the late 1950s, Terry on flugelhorn and Thelonius Monk as sideman. Some fast pieces, some ballads. A balanced, straight-on jazz mix for kids to experience.

**Threadgill, Henry,** *Where's Your Cup?* **Columbia CK 67617. Frenetic Scale: Varying, 2–10+**

Threadgill on alto sax and flute, others on guitar, accordion, harmonium, and five-string fretless bass, this is strange and exciting music. Good for an eerie journal prompt. ("The Flew," Track 5, gets *very* wild, and might be good to avoid if you have any kids on the edge.) Jazz aficionados love this CD for its fearlessness and innovation.

**Turtle Island String Quartet,** *Turtle Island String Quartet,* **Windham Hill Jazz WD-0110. Frenetic Scale: 4**

Great versions by these top-notch players: "Stolen Moments," "A Night in Tunisia," other jazz classics rendered emotively: lots of surprises. Think of Tracks 1–4 for one session, 5–8 for another, 9–15 for a third. Very different music on this CD, all of it good for journals.

**Tyner, McCoy,** *Land of Giants,* **Telarc CD 83576. Frenetic Scale: 3/4**

Really smooth stuff. Bobby Hutcherson, Charnett Moffett, and Eric Harland combine with Tyner's piano for lovely, clean jazz. Some is fast, but the group's tight cohesion renders it a nonpollutant to kids' writing. Tyner's tones worth paying attention to. Great that kids can hear the vibes in Hutcherson's hands.

**Williams, Anthony,** *Life Time,* **Blue Note 7243 4 99004 24. Frenetic Scale: 5–8**

Compelling music: moody, extemporaneous. Sam Rivers on sax, Gary Peacock on bass, Williams on drums, Herbie Hancock, Bobby Hutcherson, Ron Carter. All-star cast, great second-semester offering for writers.

**Young, Lester,** *The Definitive Lester Young,* **Verve 314–549 082–2. Frenetic Scale: 3–6**

Part of the Ken Burns Jazz series, this Young sax of the 1940s and 1950s is terrific, if a little distant in transcription. Start it anywhere; rewards to be had.

## WORLD MUSIC

**Alemañy, Jesús,** *Cubanismo!* **Root Jazz HNCD 1390. Frenetic Scale: 6**

Hard-driving CD featuring Alemañy on trumpet—he *sings*—and Paris-based Cuban pianist Alfredo Rodriguez. You can imagine this music not only in Havana but in some smoky downstairs club in Montmartre's Boulevard de Clichy. This is dance music: rumbas, cha-chas, *danzones, congas de comparsas.* Upbeat, magnificent in its rhythmics, students will write like crazy.

Note: a few cuts contain singing. Consider beginning with Cut 6. (And the authors of this book won't tell if you cut a few quick rumba steps while the kids are madly writing.)

**Aquabella, Francisco,** *Ochimini,* **Ubiquity Records CBCD042. Frenetic Scale: 6**

Master conga drummer Aquabella with high-level Afro-Cuban musicians. Familiar tunes like "Love for Sale," but lots of classic Latin rhythms.

**The Chieftains,** *The Chieftains #2,* **Claddagh Records/Atlantic 83350–2. Frenetic Scale: 5**

Did you think you didn't like Irish music? No, it's not just bad versions of the beautiful and tragic "Danny Boy," but slip jigs and airs, double jigs and reels—ah, yes, it's real: "O'Farrell's Welcome to Limerick" and "The Humours of Whiskey" await you. The kids will love this CD. *Great* writing music.

**Chinese Instrumental Ensemble,** *Masterpieces of Chinese Folksongs,* **Water Lily/ Wind SMCD 1004. Frenetic Scale: 1–2**

Yes, "easy listening," but good music, too: accomplished musicians playing classical Chinese music on the *erhu, guzheng, yangqin,* and *pipa.* The titles themselves are calming: "Purple Bamboo Melody," "The Soft Murmuring Song of a Creek," others.

**Fadl, Mahmoud,** *Love Letter from King Tut-Ank-Amen,* pi'ra:nha PIR 1257. Frenetic Scale: 7

Don't let the frenetic scale rating scare you away from this controlled, elegant CD. Nubian "master drummer of the Nile" Mahmoud Fadl combines with Samy El Bably, "Grandmaster of the Trumpet Oriental." I'd consider starting on Track 2, but anywhere you begin begets a remarkable journal session featuring music to which most students probably are not accustomed.

**Kronos Quartet,** *Pieces of Africa,* Electra Nonesuch, E2 79275. Frenetic Scale: 5

Music representing eight different African countries, often featuring African musicians working with our stellar American Kronos Quartet. I can't get enough of Track 3, and often start the CD there for Journal Time. (Track 2 includes singing, and can be distractive; I'd skip it.) Remember to come back for later tracks during other journal sessions; Tracks 7–11, comprising one symphonic piece, vibrate with energy.

**Lewiston, David (recorded by),** *Bali: Gamelan & Kecak,* Electra/Nonesuch 9 79204–2. Frenetic Scale: 6

Lewiston has chosen typical Balinese Kecak and Gamelan for this recording (part of Nonesuch's "Explorer Series"), but with a difference: these are among the best musicians in Bali. Kids who have never heard the metallophone or the Balinese jew's harp or froggy *enggung* will be in for a treat. Very optimistic music. For social studies teachers, the liner notes are worth the price of the CD itself. (Track 8, the *Kecak,* is choral and pretty wild. Worth listening to after the journal session, but *this* piece is so magnetic it'll stop students' writing.)

**de Lucia, Paco,** *Cositas Buenas,* Blue Thumb B0001939–02. Frenetic Scale: 4–7

*Nuevo Flamenco.* Paco de Lucia breaking new ground in Flamenco guitar. Great CD to give kids a sense of Flamenco rhythms and *cante hondo.* (Avoid Track 2; it has singing, would make writing difficult. De Lucia takes from different types of music (tango, rumba) and Flamenco-izes it. Laser-sharp picking here.

**Ma, Yo-Yo,** *Obrigado Brazil,* Sony Classical SK 89935. Frenetic Scale: Varying, 2–8

I resisted the idea of a Yo-Yo Ma Brazilian CD, but he won me over, and continues to amaze. This CD includes a few *very* old Brazilian classics (Villa-Lobos represented here), a little Jobim, and some newer music. Ma is virtuoso, as usual, and great for journals. (Caveat: Track 2 and Track 13, though lovely, feature vocals. Best to start at Track 3. You'll get two good sessions between the vocal tracks.)

**Markovic, Boban, Orchestra, *Live in Belgrade,* pi'ra:nha PIR 1685. Frenetic Scale: 8–9**

Here's a bet that your kids have not heard, recently at least, a big Serbian Gypsy brass band. Plenty loud, plenty of *fun,* this is a delightful CD for late spring.

**Paredes, Carlos, *Guitarra Portuguesa,* Electra/Nonesuch 9 79203–2. Frenetic Scale: 4**

Classical Portuguese guitar classics by a master. Not background guitar music by any means, but keen, clean work. Stimulating, but doesn't overexcite the kids.

**Piazzolla, Astor, *Tango: Zero Hour,* Nonesuch 79469–2. Frenetic Scale: 6**

Do you know Piazzolla? If not, this CD is a must-buy. Tracks 1, 2, and 3 go twenty minutes total, but begin it anywhere: the entire CD is exquisite and original by this Argentine *bandoneon* master and composer.

**Rampal, Jean-Pierre, and Laskine, Lily, *Sakura,* CBS MK 34568. Frenetic Scale: 2**

Traditional Japanese music (Rampal on flute, Laskine on harp) from the Meiji, Taisho, and Showa eras. East meets West: Rampal is very popular in Japan, and respected for his faithful renditions of exacting Japanese classics. The kids will enjoy this music, well-matched to an introspective prompt.

**Shankar, Ravi, *Concert for Peace,* Moment MRCD 1013. Frenetic Scale: 3**

World-renowned sitarist Shankar's concert at Royal Albert Hall. This two-CD set is great for journals. If you start the first CD about forty seconds in, you'll avoid his oral introduction of the first piece. Track 1 (twenty-two minutes) is good for an entire session; so is Track 3. Start the second CD a little over a minute in to avoid the intro. The second CD is all one track: more than fifty minutes. Contemplative work, even when the tempo gets going and the tabla's rolling.

**3 Leg Torso, *Astor in Paris,* Meester Records MEE002. Frenetic Scale: 2–7**

Yes, an *homage* to Astor Piazzolla, but far beyond. An innovative mesh of tango, modern composition, Eastern European and Middle Eastern folk, *klemish.* Some hurried and energetic work, other broody and evocative. Riveting collection, worth the kids' attention. (Track 11, "Danza Lucumi," a slow elegance.)

**Villadangos, Victor, *Guitar Music of Argentina,* Naxos 8.555058. Frenetic Scale: 2**

Exquisite music written for guitar by some of Argentina's most important composers: Pujol, Saúl, Ayala, Guastavino, Falú, and Heinze. (A little Charlie Haden influence here and there?) Seventy minutes: at least three solid journal sessions. Buenos Aires native Villadangos's work is remarkable. There's something about solo guitar that focuses kids, and you'll see that phenomenon manifest here.

**Yoshimura, Nanae, *The Art of Koto,* Volume One, Celestial Harmonies 13186–2. Frenetic Scale: 1**

It's not possible to get less frenetic than this, unless we play gelid New-Age massage music. Yoshimura is one of Japan's premier *koto* (long zither) players, and the classical pieces found on this CD originate from between the seventeenth and nineteenth centuries. (Two of the cuts have low-toned chants in them, but will distract the kids only very briefly.) Highly recommended for quiet days or days in which you want the music to focus the class quickly.

# Fifty Tips for Success from Students

For most students who have never practiced sustained spontaneous writing, keeping the ideas flowing and the pen moving may seem an impossible task. When energy and motivation ebb, we've found it useful for students to share tricks they use to keep writing. They've come up with many more clever tips than we imagined. Ask *your* students to share what they do to write a page and a half in twenty minutes. When they run out of ideas, we invite you to use what Jerry's students have suggested.

### How Do You Get Started?

1. Read the prompt carefully and *really* understand it.

2. Start by writing whatever you know about the topic—then ideas will flow.

3. Write as if you're talking to someone.

4. First think of answers to how/what/when/where/why it happened.

5. Pretend you are there, then write what you see.

6. First brainstorm what you're going to write about.

### How Do You Know *What* to Write About?

7. Write what's on your mind.

8. Journal Time is a great time to reflect on your past or write about your family, friends, school, issues in your life.

9. Write about something that just happened or what happens in other classes.

10. Write the first thing that comes to mind.

11. Write a folk tale.

12. Write about something you're interested in or feel strongly about.

13. Tell a story.

14. Write about something you know, like music or family.

15. Write stories you've dreamed about.

16. Write about something random and write random things about it.

17. Write what you want to say (but can't say) to your friends.

18. If you are angry at something, write as much as you can and let your anger go.

**How Do You Write a *Lot?***

19. Go into great detail.

20. Don't leave anything out.

21. Think of all related topics.

22. Use big words (which use more space and can help you write longer).

23. Start writing while the student is reading the topic!

24. It's good to have a central idea that you can go back to every time you get stuck or run out of ideas on one branch. Usually that central idea is your title.

25. Try to "say" your journal to yourself before you write every single word.

26. Ask questions, then answer them.

27. The key word is *imagination.*

28. Write full answers to every question.

29. Write about the big picture, then take it apart and put in details.

30. Take it section by section.

31. Talk about what is common and related to the topic, then give examples.

32. Don't restrain yourself from any ideas.

33. Don't put down your pen or play with it—that will distract you.

34. Keep thinking that you're not writing enough to write more.

35. Use more than one sentence to answer each question.

36. Write the first paragraph (introduction) and then you know what to write next.

37. "Stretch" an idea into many sentences.

38. Time yourself: within 15 minutes, try to have at least 3/4 of the paper filled.

39. Use the topic as a guide but write a story—make up characters.

40. Answer the first question to get you started, then go on your own and write whatever comes to mind.

41. Put dialogue in your story.

42. Answer *every* question in the prompt.

43. Make a connection between the topic and yourself.

44. Make up questions about the topic and answer them.

45. Write about how the topic affects others.

46. Try to write the whole time and don't stop until the time is up.

47. Have an open mind, wide imagination, stay focused, and write fast.

48. Keep a little black book of words that come to mind. Whenever you write, you can go back to that little black book.

49. The introduction is the hardest part to write—I like to compare what I'm going to write to something else.

50. Make an outline—it makes it really easy to sort out ideas into different paragraphs.

# Taxonomy of Teacher Comments on Individual Journal Entries

| Comment | | | Purpose |
|---|---|---|---|
| **WOW!**<br>**Thank You**<br>**Aha!**<br>**Smart**<br>**Terrific**<br>**Funny**<br>**Such a**<br>**great intro**<br>**I'm glad, A.** | **COOL!**<br>**So Great!**<br>**I agree**<br>**Yes!**<br>**So true**<br>**I love it**<br>**This is valuable**<br>**to me, C.** | **Good!**<br>**SUPER!**<br>**OK**<br>**Good stuff, Eva.**<br>**Great**<br>**Lovely**<br>**You're a good**<br>**writer, Bobby!**<br>**Right—I think so** | **Validate, encourage,**<br>**acknowledge, reward** |
| **I've seen a strong difference.**<br>**Yes!**<br>**I hope so.** | | | **Respond to content;**<br>**answer questions** |
| **The reason I do that is to get kids**<br>**to develop their topics, J.** | | | **Explain, clarify** |
| **Grammar mistake circled**<br>**Correct spelling of misspelled word** | | | **Indicate language**<br>**mistakes (very occasional)** |
| **This is a good *start*, but I want you to really**<br>**concentrate on longer entries, OK?**<br><br>**So short, Mike! I love your ideas—**<br>**but I want *more* of them!** | | | **Nudge, push** |
| **I appreciate the good feedback, A.**<br>**Good to get your opinion, D.**<br>**That is good to know, D.**<br>**Thanks, K.** | | | **Conclude** |
| **But you're such a good writer!**<br>**You *have* improved!**<br>**Your writing has improved so much, W.** | | | **Evaluate** |

# Student Examples

## 1. PAMELA'S END-OF-YEAR ENTRY

In this late-May writing, Pamela reflects on her first reaction to Fluency Journals and how she changed. She claims that steady writing was easy from the beginning, but that she became more open-minded and more persuasive, and that her confidence increased!

## 2. YA NI'S END-OF-YEAR ENTRY

For this second-language learner, the journal writing was difficult at first, but Ya Ni remarks that it got easier as the year progressed. Writing in such volume makes her proud.

## 3. TIM'S ADVICE

Tim's writing points to the importance of allowing students to select their own topics. He loves writing about what he calls "random things," but as you read his entry, you'll see that he chooses to write about his interests. Tim has a great sense of audience and uses his journal to be playful. (Jerry reports that although many of Tim's entries were "eccentric and quirky," he nonetheless devoted the entire Journal Time to intense, concentrated writing.)

## 4. ANGELA'S JOURNAL STRATEGIES

This journal entry is superb, not only in its advice on how to succeed with *Rain, Steam, and Speed*, but also as an excellent model for students. Angela has done a fine job of organizing main ideas in paragraphs and developing her points through explanation and examples. She did this in a little over twenty minutes!

## 5. JERRY XIE'S PRE AND POST ENTRIES

These two journal entries, one written in early September and the other in late May, show growth in the variety of ideas, the complexity of language, and the amount of writing. The early sample relates a sequential list of events and fills three-quarters of a page. Many of the sentences begin in the same way (*Then I asked . . . There I hear . . .*). The late sample reflects a much more confident writer through the use of adverbs such as *Frankly, certainly, actually,* and weaves a variety of writing strategies (examples, quotations, reason, explanations) throughout this much longer entry to support varied (but related) ideas. Jerry is able, too, to assert his new "voice" in teasing the teacher, referring to his long-running commentary during the year about that "scary" music (see the music of Gloria Coates, Appendix A), which he'd never experienced before.

## Pamela's End-of-Year Entry

May 27, 2003

Journals

I think that this whole Journal experience was a good one. In the beginning of it all, I was not at all, overwhelmed. I was very happy actually. The reason being because I had so many ideas for it. I hadn't written or expressed myself to a teacher about random things before. I never took the time to focus on those things . . . it's like those topics are in the back of my head. I really enjoyed writing about things like 3rd world countries, the Debate between Public & Private Schools, and things like that. It just felt so good to finally get it off my chest and to have someone listen was such an experience. I mean let's face it, it's not like those kind of things pop up in friendly conversation. I thought I would do extremely well because of the quality of my ideas & the quantity of things I had to support my idea. The first few weeks were a breeze, but later on, I don't know why, I didn't dig journal writing as much as I used to. It's like the cave was empty. I ran out of things to say. I talked about all the ideas I had already.

I think my writing has become more advanced over the year. I have become more open minded & quite persuasive (I think ☺). I noticed I write a bit more now.

Relaxation is is great in the classroom, sometimes a bit too relaxing that I sometimes drift off! I have a lot more confidence than I did before, but my confidence in reading my work will always stay the same . . . I'll never really be cured from that. This journal helps you find out who you are as a person, because you can never find out who you are unless you write it on paper & re-evaluate everything.

To improve journal writing, there should be more time, about 35 minutes. Journals should be on Mondays & Fridays. I am extremely proud of the quality & quantity I have written during the whole year.

# Ya Ni's End-of-Year Entry

|  |  |
|---|---|
| Journal Entry | May 27, 2003 |

Well, this is the last journal of they year for me. A little ☹. It's been really great writing these journals. In my whole life, I never wrote this much journals before. This really helped me a lot in writing.

When the process was explained, I thought it was a really good idea. And I really think that it would help me a lot. But I didn't really think that I would do really in this since I'm a really bad writer. The first few weeks the were a bit of struggle for me, but later on when I got use to it, it turned pretty easy for me. So now I think my writing had change to a little better, at least better than before.

In the writings that I've done before, I mostly write about my self. But as the year went by, I started to write about other stuff or people. But the grammar and sentence structures, I'm still really bad at it.

I really need big help from other people about my grammar and sentence structures. But when ever I read or proof read other people's papers, I can tell their grammar errors and all these other problems out, but just cant for myself.

Well, what you've been doing for the journal entries is really good. Putting music out so we can relax while writing our journal. But one thing is that, don't so much of the exciting or scary music out, because exciting and scary music will be rushing, thinking that the time is rushing by too. Mostly play soft and quiet music. I think the time limit is a little bit too short.

It should be like 30 minutes. And I think you should do the journals more often because, it seems like you stopped for a while. The topics are really good since mostly it's optional.

And finally I'm really proud of the amount of writing I'm doing, Thank you Mr. Fleming.

Todays Weather:

SUNNY

Days til graduation:
9 Days!

Days till Roberts Park:
2 Days!

Days till Graduation Dinner Dance:
6 Days!

(10 minutes)

March 4, 2003

### Strategies

I do not have many strategies for writing in my journal. I just randomly think of something random and write random things about it. I do not understand how, but all of this randomness turns out to be a very humerous experience. I call it . . . Skillz. I was born with the gifted ability to be able to say random things at random times, and still have things to back up the randomness.

*Funny*

It is really very easy to write in my journal. I just think of something random, such as shampoo, and keep on writing about how shampoo would make a hobo's life much easier and better. Or for instance if I feel like I'm in a "Hippy" mood, I will write about how my mom and dad were tree hugging hippies.

*it's Tim.*

Another strategy I have is to not have any strategy at all and just write whatever I feel should be on paper and known. A good example of this is, my "The hobos are coming" stories. I know that they will come someday, and I know that humanitys only hope will be the squirrels. This will all happen someday, so I might as well write about it to warn our future. The attack could be now . . . The attack could be now . . . Oh yea, the attack could even be now . . . Or will it be next Tuesday? The world may never know.

Sometimes, I will write on the topic that Mr. Flemming puts on the board. I only do this either when the topic is of interest to me, or when I am fresh out of 'good' or funny ideas to share with the world. I really hate these days because they really limit my creativity as a human being. Let the creativity live on!!! I really hate when people try to stop my creativity.

ok,
Tim.

March 4, 2003

*Journal Strategies*

Here's some advice on writing journals that I use to maximizing my writing. First off, write what you care about! You can't go very far if you write something you have no care for. Instead of writing about your brother's boring and weird day (which I have no care for), why not write about something you strongly feel about. Your opinion on a topic, like basketball or the death penalty.

My second strategy is to ask and brainstorm some questions in your mind. How does it feel like to fly? What happens after death? Then, you get to write all your thoughts, concoctions, inventions, imaginations, and dream. You can right about the news that day and your thoughts. In journals, you must always include your thoughts, feelings, your soul! I think so because journals are all about knowing the writer, discovering the writer's motives.

Another strategy is to write about something that inspires you. Or write whenever you have an inspiration. Inspirations are slippery like water, so whenever you get one, be sure to jot it down for a journal topic!

You can always use big words that take up a lot of space and make you sound like a college professor. Whenever you learn new words, expand that vocabulary sack in your brain, and use it!

To lengthen your writing, you should use a lot of details. Details always make writing longer, more interesting, more elegant, and fun! So instead of writing: today, I went to eat at McDonald's, write something like: I took the cable car to Chinatown McDonald's and when I entered, there was a grey-cloud colored pigeon bobbing and clucking around. It was funny when the workers who wore scarlet uniforms tried to chase the pigeon off the high roost on the door ledge. It was not funny, however, when the pigeon gave me a globby and much unappreciated gift. What I've just done was stretch one sentence into a few, because I wrote down details, thoughts, and every observation. That's what a writer does too, observe!

You can also lengthen your writing by breaking the writing dam and just let your mind flow through your arm and out your pencil. Never stop or falter, or you'll forget the thought and let the flood of writing potentials overwhelm you! By letting your mind flow, you are not restrained from telling the reader about you and writing a good journal!

Another strategy is to talk to your reader and communicate through your writing. This makes your writing more animated and lively. Your writing would be more spruced up than it would be if you just wrote about something in text book style. No connection with the reader at all. Who wants to read something from a text book other than to study?

The last strategy I'm giving you is this: use literary devises. You should use metaphors, similes, hyperboles, personification, etc. To make this sentence longer: The building is green, you can use a simile. The building is green like the emerald color of a peacock feather. See? I made the sentence longer.

One last thing, have fun when writing journals. You can't write long without motivation. So if you are not having fun or any motivation, stop, and write your journal topic in a style that would be fun for you. You can write in letter style, diary style, news article style, feature style, review style, or any other creative style you could think of.

So, that's all I can think of right now. Gotta go.

*Jerry — a good start; your full twenty-minute journal will be great.*

September 11, 2002

## My Memorys of September 11th

*So scary.*

When I first heard of the first plane crashing into the first tower, I was on the bus. Kids suddenly started saying something about no school. Then I asked a friend what was going on. He said that a plane hit something in New York. Then I said is there going to be no school then, he said yes.

*Lucky!*

In luck, I found my mom right when I got off the bus. I told her that a plane hit something in New York and I went straight for home. As soon as I got home I turned on the television. There I heard the news reporter say that Flight something hit one of the World Trade Centers. I was shocked in disbelief. Not long after that, the news reporter said that another plane hit the

*an amazing, shocking day, J.*

second tower. They showed us a clip that a person took. It was unbelieveable. A plane hit the first WTC. Then it went up in flames. Then the other clip, the other plane hitting the other tower.

As I watched, I was in disbelief and in a cyclone of confusion. Soon after, the twin towers collasped. The first time in my life that I have ever saw such a tragic event.

May 27, 2003

<u>Last Journal Entry</u>

Since this is the last journal entry of the year, lets make it memorable.

Anyway, in the beginning, when it all started I loved it. But, it was one of those things that you love but can't really live up to. Frankly it was actually really hard when it first showed up as a grade. It was certainly a struggle. A hundred percent sure that it was a struggle. It wasn't easy at all. You had to write a page and a half in twenty minutes.

As the process of journal went on, it actually got easier. I notice myself writing more as time went by. First it was 3/4's of a page. Then it went up to a page (a little more from time to time). Finally, it was a page and a half. I saw myself write more and more as time went on. And soon as I wrote more, I went on to my favorite topics. Then I wrote even more! Journal is definitely going to a memerble experience.

My attitude towards Journal changed from "ehh, okay" to "Oh heck yeah!" Now I love journal time. One of the reasons I love journal time is because you can write your mind down in a little piece of paper. The good part is that you wont get arrested or yelled at for doing that.

I noticed that my journal length greatly rose. Like I told

you, from 3/4 a page to one and a half. Now while writing journal, I'm more relaxed. Before it was oh no I'm not going to get it done. Now its, relax, let your hand do the work.

If I'm sure about one thing, I'm sure that journal gave me a sense of who I really am. Want me to tell you? Sure I'm a funny tall guy with attitude. Get it? Got it? Good.

Well Mr. Fleming, if you have something to improve about journal time. It's gotta be the music. I'm not saying it's bad, but I'm not saying it's not. The music you put on is kind of scary.

One thing about Journals depend on is well, time. And more time is what we need. I'm sure I need more time to express myself on the cool topics. But for the not so interesting journal topics, less time is cool.

Talking about topics, they're great. I loved it when we had that journal entry on which superhero would you want to be, and the entry on what your going to be when you grow up. I also like the million dollar question (what would you do if you had a million). Remember?

Anyway, I'm going to miss journal time. A lot! I'm also going to miss you Mr. Fleming. Peace!

# Bibliography

Bartholomae, D. "Teaching Basic Writing: An Alternative to Basic Skills." In G. DeLuca, L. Fox, M.-A. Johnson, and M. Kogen (eds.), *Dialogue on Writing.* Hillsdale, N.J.: Erlbaum, 2002.

Burton, J., and Carroll, J. (eds.). *Journal Writing.* Alexandria, Va.: Teachers of English to Speakers of Other Languages, 2001.

Campbell, C. *Teaching Second-Language Writing: Interacting with Text.* Boston: Heinle & Heinle, 1998.

Flower, L. *Problem-Solving Strategies for Writing.* Orlando, Fla.: Harcourt Brace, 1981.

Heard, G. *The Revision Toolbox: Teaching Techniques That Work.* Portsmouth, N.H.: Heinemann, 2002.

Ponsot, M., and Deen, R. *Beat Not the Poor Desk.* Portsmouth, N.H.: Heinemann, 1982.

Progoff, I. *At a Journal Workshop.* New York: Dialogue House Library, 1975.

Smith, M., and Wilhelm, J. *Reading Don't Fix No Chevys.* Portsmouth, N.H.: Heinemann, 1998.

# INDEX

CPSIA information can be obtained at www.ICGtesting.com
Printed in the USA
BVOW09s0919270415

397621BV00005B/9/P